Kathy Willis is Director of Scie <barcode> KT-382-484 Kew. She is also Professor of Biodiversity and a fellow of Merton College, both at Oxford University. Winner of several awards, she has spent over twenty-five years researching and teaching bio-diversity and conservation at Oxford and Cambridge.

Carolyn Fry is a freelance science writer. She has written seven successful books, including *Plant Hunters*, winner of the European Garden Book Prize. Formerly Editor of the Royal Geographical Society's magazine, *Geographical*, her work has been published in *New Scientist*, BBC Online, *Telegraph*, *Guardian*, *The Times* and *Independent on Sunday*.

'A fascinating portrait' *Sunday Times*

'Lavished with beautiful, never-before-seen photographs and illustrations, this book offers something for everyone – drama, adventure, history, science and innovation. A must-read' *BBC Country File*

'Lively, thought-provoking and scholarly' *Garden Design*

'An aesthetic, historical and scientific journey through the flowering of botany as a science. This beautifully illustrated book, replete with botanical plates, scientific engravings and fine photographs, is nearly as much of a treat as a visit to the gardens' *New Scientist*

ROYAL BOTANIC GARDENS

BBC
RADIO 4

PLANTS

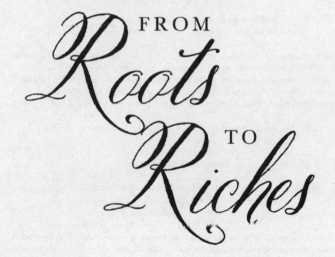

FROM

Roots

TO

Riches

KATHY WILLIS and CAROLYN FRY

JOHN MURRAY

First published in Great Britain in 2014 by John Murray (Publishers)
An Hachette UK Company

First published in paperback in 2015

1

A CIP catalogue record for this title is available from the British Library

ISBN 978-1-444-79825-8
Ebook ISBN 978-1-444-79824-1

Typeset in Garamond by Palimpsest Book Production Ltd, Falkirk, Stirlingshire

Printed and bound by Clays Ltd, St Ives plc

John Murray policy is to use papers that are natural, renewable and recyclable products
and made from wood grown in sustainable forests. The logging and manufacturing processes are
expected to conform to the environmental regulations of the country of origin.

John Murray (Publishers)
Carmelite House
50 Victoria Embankment
London EC4Y 0DZ

www.johnmurray.co.uk

The BOTANIC MACARONI

CONTENTS

vii

PREFACE

Plants were here first. They first colonised our oceans a staggering 3,800 million years ago. Later, when the land emerged from the waters, plants came too, carpeting the surface of the earth with a thin, fragile layer of green from around 480 million years ago. The earliest humans gained their first tentative toeholds here a mere two million years ago.

There are more of them than us. There are thought to be approximately half a million plant species compared to just one species of modern human. In terms of total mass of organically bound carbon, there is also no contest – on land, there is about 1,000 times more plant than animal biomass.

We need them. Plants provide our air, food, clothing, shelter, fuel, medicine, means of transport and ways of storing knowledge. They contribute the basic raw materials for everything we do, and have carried on supplying this limitless fecundity whatever we have chosen to throw at them – at least so far. We need to know where this amazing, uncomplaining generosity comes from, how it works, and how we can preserve it and stop damaging it by negligence, accident or deliberate fault.

It is perhaps rather surprising, then, given the importance of plants on earth, that we only started to study them as an academic discipline fewer than 200 years ago. Botany, as it was known, is still a relative newcomer at the top table of science, and it had to work hard to earn its place. Much of that work was done here, at the Royal Botanic Gardens at Kew, on an elegant bend of the slow-moving river Thames, some ten miles to the west of the centre of London.

Kew Gardens was founded in 1759 by Princess Augusta, who was married to Frederick Prince of Wales, eldest son of King George II. The 300 acres (121 hectares) of gracious parkland owe their survival amidst the spread of the smart London suburbs to their status as a royal park and favourite leisure ground, so that once botany became a proper science, Kew was ready to receive it and became its ideal home. The concept of the botanic garden, part public park, part scientific research facility, was born. Its descendants have sprung up all over the world, forming a unique network of plant life on earth in all its variety and splendour.

Today there are more than 300 scientists at Kew, from taxonomists who name things and systematists who compare things, to conservationists, plant health experts and researchers, whose work spills over into politics and economics through the study of land use, plant natural capital and food. The science, of course, has changed beyond recognition in the 250 years since Kew was founded, with rapid advances in the understanding of, for example, molecular biology, and the technology to exploit it. But the questions scientists have been trying to answer have remained roughly the same.

The first plant scientists were genuine pioneers. Often they worked against prejudice and indifference. Botany wasn't a real science. At best it was seen as a Cinderella discipline, fit for gentlemen and ladies of leisure, dabbling in their gardens. Most great botanists started out as something else – gardeners or engineers, sometimes even monks and priests. They were regarded as eccentrics, their company tolerated on expeditions of conquest and discovery (as Joseph Banks's was on Captain Cook's first voyage), but no more. There are some remarkable characters among these frontier scientists, and stories of triumph and of tragedy. Some, of course, found themselves barking up the wrong tree, or even scraping at the wrong bark. But the real characters are the plants themselves, from the orchid that looks like a bee to the waterlily big enough to walk on. They exerted a powerful fascination that has inspired at once a quest for knowledge about their science, a cultural interest in taming, growing and (often) eating plants from the furthest corners of the Empire, and a passion to understand and witness these monstrous wonders, these compelling curiosities.

A great scientist once said that the important thing is not simply to accumulate facts, but to ask challenging questions and to seek to answer them. Some of the greatest challenges on earth today – climate change (and in particular increasing atmospheric carbon dioxide), population growth, food security and disease – are intimately connected to our symbiotic relationship with plants. Plants will certainly provide at least some of the solutions. The terminology and the scale may have changed: we can probably afford to believe that we will never again allow an entire country to starve because of lack of understanding of genetic diversity (as happened in Ireland in the 1850s). But, when reading this book, it is remarkable how often we find scientists, now long dead, asking the same questions that we are still asking today: how do plants pass on their most useful characteristics from one generation to the next? Ask Gregor Mendel, peering at his peas. What happens when politics overrides scientific freedom? Look at the tragedy of Nikolai Vavilov's team, starving to death in a freezing basement during the siege of Leningrad to protect the precious specimens that would go on to help feed millions.

This book provides a unique examination of the emergence of the academic discipline of botany; a timeline in the development of the subject from its first beginnings through to the present day. It focuses on the major breakthroughs in botanical knowledge over the past 200 years and places them within their historical context as seen through the lens of the Royal Botanic Gardens at Kew. In some cases Kew was the institution leading the scientific break-through, in others it was responding to work elsewhere. Kew has always provided a central clearing-house for both ideas and speci-mens from all corners of the natural and the intellectual world.

And it still does. This is a story that is still going on. There may not be quite as many grey beards and waistcoats as in the days of Kew's band of botanical eccentrics and fanatics, but the scientists are still here. Its past Director Joseph Hooker and his contemporary George Bentham would surely have been deeply satisfied that their passionate belief in the importance of plants, and their ideas about how to learn from them, are still at the heart of what Kew does today.

We need those ideas now more than ever.

Kathy Willis
June 2014

I

A ROSE BY ANY OTHER NAME

Portrait of Carl Linnaeus from his major work *Systema Naturae*,
1748 edition

WALK THROUGH THE main gate into Kew Gardens and you can't miss the Palm House: a glass cathedral to plants. At its southern end stands one of Kew's most ancient residents. It's a cycad, a palm-like tree, its bark patterned in a mosaic of diamond shapes that give it the appearance of an alligator as it winds several metres up towards the domed glass roof, eventually shooting out a crown of dark glossy fronds. Although not a thing of obvious beauty, this cycad is astonishing and remarkable for a number of reasons. For one thing, it belongs to a group of plants with extraordinary longevity. Cycads, which bear cones and are related to conifers, have been around for 280 million years. They've survived multiple climate changes, outliving the dinosaurs, and they predate most flowering plants and mammals.

This particular exhibit is also remarkable because it's probably older than Kew Gardens; it is one of the oldest pot plants in the world, not to mention being more ancient than the system of naming plants as we currently know it. It is hard to believe but the plant has been at the Gardens since 1775, a year before the United States of America was founded. It flourished as the last stages of the Little Ice Age froze parts of the nearby river Thames, as the Napoleonic Wars raged and when the first ever journey was made by steam locomotive. In its day, it would have kept company with the likes of King George III, Queen Victoria and Charles Darwin. It has been an evergreen witness to Kew's role in the evolution of botany from a gentleman's hobby to a scientific profession of international significance, supported by governments and organisations worldwide, tackling critical issues that affect the global economy and the conservation of our planet.

This plant, *Encephalartos altensteinii*, is a native of South Africa. It was among some 500 specimens brought to Kew by the Gardens' first ever plant collector, Francis Masson. Under particular instructions from Joseph Banks, Kew's de facto Director, Masson dug up the young cycad in 1773 in the rainforests of the Eastern Cape. Its voyage – overland, by ship to the Port of London, then by boat along the Thames to Kew – took some two years. Its safe arrival would have pleased King George III's mother, Princess Augusta, had she still been alive. She had wished the Gardens to 'contain all the plants known on Earth' when she founded them in 1759.

By the late eighteenth century, as Kew's prize cycad was settling into its pot, the practice of botany had already been established in the West for more than two thousand years. The scientific study of plants dates back to ancient Greece, when the philosopher and scientist Theophrastus, a pupil of Aristotle, published the earliest surviving treatises. In the nine surviving volumes of *Enquiry into Plants* and the six volumes of *Causes of Plants*, dating to about 300 BC, he describes around 500 plants from the Mediterranean and beyond, noting the characteristics of varieties of trees, shrubs, herbaceous plants and cereals, as well as investigating the juices of plants and their medicinal uses. In his introduction, Theophrastus examines how plants are to be classified, mentioning the difficulty in identifying and defining their essential components. Much of the information he included on Greek plants clearly came from his own observations. His approach was surprisingly modern; pondering whether parts of plants correspond directly with those of animals, and questioning whether flowers, catkins, leaves and fruit should be considered constituents of a plant, given their apparently short lifespan within that of the plant itself.

Theophrastus is often called the 'father of botany' because so much of his work foreshadows our modern study of plants. Not only did he apply systematic techniques of observation, but he also created botanical terms to facilitate discussion, and pioneered the use of hierarchical systems of names. His interests extended to all aspects of the plant world, such as the relationship between plant distribution and climate. A further parallel with botany as it was to develop in Victorian Britain was his emphasis on useful plants, with much information gathered on their medicinal and horticultural aspects. However, Theophrastus was clearly aiming

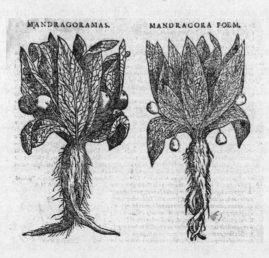

The mandrake, from a facsimile edition of Dioscorides'
De Materia Medica, 1586

to arrive at a full understanding of plants, rather than simply a practical manual.

Many of the botanical texts that followed focused on the role of plants in medicine. In AD 50, Dioscorides, who was believed to be a Roman army doctor, listed 650 species with curative properties in his *De Materia Medica*, a volume of tried and tested information that was widely consulted for the next 1,500 years. By the fifteenth century, botanists had developed elementary classification systems and were knowledgeable about the properties of a wide range of flora. By this time gardens of medicinal plants, or 'gardens of simples', were often found in monasteries and medical schools. The sixteenth century saw the more systematic development of what came to be called the physic garden. These were first established at Pisa in 1544 and at Padua in 1545, but further gardens soon sprang up in Florence, Bologna, Leiden, Paris and Oxford. As early as 1555, the Spanish royal physician Andrés Laguna was trying to persuade his king that 'All the princes and universities of Italy take pride in having many excellent gardens, adorned with all kinds of plants found throughout the world, and so it is most proper that Your Majesty provide and order that we have at least one in Spain, sustained with royal stipends.'

Initially, these physic gardens were quite small. Flower beds were laid out in formal geometric patterns, with plants arranged according to aesthetic and symbolic considerations. By 1600, more practical arrangements based on geography or species were the norm. The gardens were closely linked to medical schools, providing a place where apprentice apothecaries could learn how to recognise plants and prepare drugs. Much emphasis was given to the accurate naming of the plants in physic gardens – it was vital for their medicinal use. This led to the contemporary establishment of herbaria (collections of pressed plants mounted on sheets of paper).

The physic garden at Padua, established in 1545

In many respects the modern botanical garden such as Kew – made up of collections of living plants, pressed plants and books – is a direct descendant of the original physic garden.

It wasn't long, however, before the role of the physic gardens shifted from growing medicinal plants to showcasing exotics. As the world opened up following the pioneering voyages of Christopher Columbus to the Americas and Vasco da Gama to India, more and more plants, newly discovered, began to arrive on European shores. Botanical knowledge had soon developed to the extent that the English naturalist John Ray could list 17,000 specimens in his book *Historia Plantarum Generalis*, published in 1686.

Nevertheless, he and his contemporaries still faced Theophrastus' problem of how best to classify and name the new plants they encountered. Ray was one of a number of botanists in the late seventeenth century whose work led to the classification of plants by species, genus and family that is the basis of modern botany. The son of a village blacksmith, he was assisted by his local vicar to study at the University of Cambridge. He travelled extensively throughout Europe, collecting plants from many localities. He gave much thought to which characteristics could best be used to separate species and other plant groups, preferring features that were 'essential' – in other words stable and unchanging, such as the flowers and seeds – rather than those 'accidental' characteristics such as variations in size or smell. Like other great botanists, Ray had wide interests, and also made important contributions to understanding the inner workings of plants: plant physiology. His *Historia Plantarum* has been described as the first textbook of modern botany.

While much progress had been made in classifying plants, the assorted, often long, names being applied to the same plant were a major obstacle to further work. A single name for a daisy might comprise three lines of Latin descriptors. And a plant might have various names using the same words but in different orders simply because botanists disagreed over whether it was more important to say 'prickly leaved' or 'red flowered' first. As author and historian of science, Jim Endersby, explains:

Names were a source of great confusion. Every director of a botanic garden, every collector and student of plants had their own system. It was impossible to know how many species there were because no two experts would agree; no two used the same system. Given this botanical Tower of Babel, there was a very real sense in which no two botanists knew what they were talking about when they corresponded with one another. Each would have not only their own local names, but in many cases their own scholarly system as well, and they would often be speaking or writing in different languages, too.

One man was acutely aware of this problem. Passionate about plants, the Swedish naturalist Carl Linnaeus had been exploring, collecting and recording the plant life of his native country from his early childhood. Linnaeus's father was a curate and a keen gardener; family stories record that he decorated his baby son's cradle with flowers and would lay the child on the grass with a flower in his hand. The boy went on to study medicine, eventually becoming a professor at Uppsala University, Sweden. Linnaeus made important contributions to medicine, particularly through his interest in nutrition as preventative medicine, and by his pioneering medical anthropology among the Sami people of Lapland. However, his fame is based on his work in naming plants and animals.

Linnaeus was concerned about the future of Sweden, worrying that his nation's lack of empire, reliance on imported goods and the decadence of its ruling class would bankrupt the country. A new source of wealth was needed. It seemed to him that the answer lay in the waves of plants arriving on European shores from British, French, Spanish, Portuguese and Dutch colonies. If exotic commodities, such as tea, rice and coconuts, could be grown in Sweden, he reasoned, his nation could become self-sufficient. The possibility that plants from tropical regions might not thrive in the chilly Swedish climate did not seem to occur to him. 'If coconuts should chance to come into my hands it would be as if fried birds of paradise flew into my mouth when I opened it,' he enthused.

It is no coincidence that both Theophrastus and Linnaeus took a strong interest in economic botany, for the study of useful plants has always been central to the study of botany. In part this was because of the close link between medicine and botany in an age when most medicines were directly derived from plants. Many European botanists from the seventeenth to the nineteenth centuries trained originally in medicine; among them were Linnaeus, Darwin and Kew's Joseph Hooker.

Linnaeus's two great contributions to botany were the development of a workable classification system that could be applied to all plants (and to other organisms), and the creation of the modern system of naming plants by genus and species rather than long phrases. Both enabled the many new species being discovered on eighteenth-century voyages of discovery to be easily classified and named. Up until this point botany had been an enthusiasm for the rich: as an impoverished student Linnaeus had difficulty accessing the botanical literature of the time. It is surely no coincidence that Linnaeus published his methodologies as affordable handbooks, making them easily accessible to the novice or part-time botanist.

In his work *Systema Naturae* (*The System of Nature*), published in 1735 when he was only twenty-seven, Linnaeus set out a five-tier hierarchy for plants: of classes, orders, genera, species and varieties. He identified twenty-three classes of flowering plants according to the number and relative lengths of the male organs (stamens), which he termed 'husbands'. *Monandria*, such as *Canna*, had one stamen and were described as being like 'one husband in a marriage'; *Diandria*, such as *Veronica*, had two stamens and were said to have 'two husbands in one marriage' and so on. Linnaeus's twentieth class, *Polyandria*, which included the poppy (*Papaver*), was akin to 'twenty males or more in bed with the same female'. He added a twenty-fourth class, *Cryptogamia*, to account for plants such as mosses that didn't appear to have sexual organs. Linnaeus further divided the classes into orders, on the basis of their female sexual organs.

The classification prompted uproar in some quarters over its

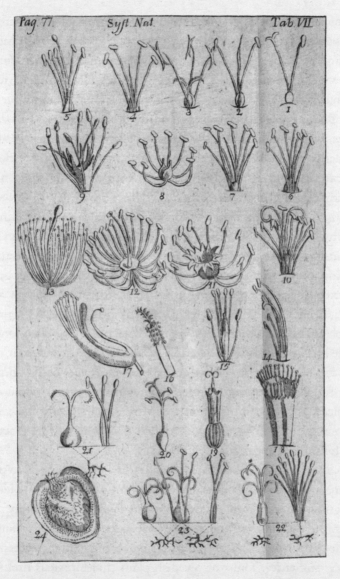

Illustration from Linnaeus's influential text *Systema Naturae*,
1748 edition

use of sexual terms (botany, after all, had thus far been regarded as a safe pastime for genteel young ladies). 'A literal translation of the first principles of Linnaean botany is enough to shock female modesty,' thundered the clergyman Samuel Goodenough, who became Bishop of Carlisle. 'It is possible that many virtuous students might not be able to make out the similitude of [the class] *Clitoria*.' Despite this opposition, and the fact that the system created 'artificial' relationships between plants, based solely on floral characteristics, it was highly practical. Keen botanists could now quickly classify their specimens.

What of the cumbersome form of botanical names, written as lengthy Latin phrases? Having honed his system for classifying organisms, Linnaeus then came up with a two-worded (binomial) naming system, of genus and species. He interpreted a genus as a group of species possessing similarly constructed flowers and fruit. Meanwhile, he considered a species name should distinguish the plant from all others of the genus. Now plant names no longer needed to be exhaustively descriptive. Following his system, if you had the name for the genus and the species, you could simply look up the description. Under this regime, a plant's name did not need to confer information about the species; instead it could honour the person who first described it or refer to the place it was found, for example.

In 1753, Linnaeus published *Species Plantarum* (*The Species of Plants*), using his new binomial classification to name 6,000 plants, alongside a description of each. Owing to their workability, his systems of classification and naming soon became the most favoured methods used in botanical works, in turn making botany accessible to new audiences. Thus the Swedish plant that Linnaeus tirelessly promoted as a local substitute for expensive China tea, the twin-flower, was named *Linnaea borealis*. As he himself wrote: 'The botanist is (therefore), distinguished from the layman in that he can give a name which fits one particular plant and not another, and which can be understood by anyone all the world over.'

It is thanks to Linnaeus that Kew's elderly cycad has, like every other animal and plant, a scientific name in two parts. Its genus name *Encephalartos* is derived from the Greek and means 'bread in the head' (this refers to the traditional practice of removing the starchy pith from the cycad's stem and kneading it into dough). Its species name, *altensteinii*, meanwhile, honours the nineteenth-century German chancellor Karl vom Stein zum Altenstein. What Linnaeus had devised was not just a way of naming living things but a way of understanding them and putting them into a stand-ardised hierarchy that he hoped would help uncover the machinery of nature. Armed with Linnaeus's system of naming, Victorian naturalists now had a grammar for plants; a language for flowers.

2

PLANTS TO SHAPE SOCIETY

Banksia serrata; native to Australia, collected by Joseph Banks
and named after him

BENEATH THE FEET of the tourists and office workers who throng London's Piccadilly lies a high-security vault. Installed in 1969, the strong room is protected by two doors, the outer a heavy Chubb and an internal one of wood, which together create an airlock. Just inside, a machine constantly records the temperature and humidity, so staff can see if either climbs too high. Yet the 4-metre by 5-metre, windowless safe contains neither money nor jewellery, as its prestigious location might suggest, but treasures of another kind.

Lining the mahogany shelves and hidden in rows of drawers are Carl Linnaeus's library and herbarium. These consist of glass-lidded boxes containing thousands of butterflies, beetles and shells; more than 14,000 dried plant specimens in folders tied up with ribbon; Linnaeus's manuscripts, penned in his diminutive script; and original copies of his influential texts *Systema Naturae* and *Species Plantarum*.

Given that Linnaeus was Swedish and spent most of his life in his homeland, it is somewhat surprising that his physical legacy lies in the UK. In fact, this came about almost by accident.

After the great man's death in 1778 at the age of seventy, the collection passed to his wife, Sara Lisa. Wanting to ensure that the collection would be safeguarded, she contacted Joseph Banks, who happened to be having breakfast with the young naturalist

James Edward Smith when he opened her letter. Banks suggested that purchasing the collection would help to make the younger man's name in the world of science.

So, with the initially reluctant help of his father, a wealthy wool merchant, Smith acquired Linnaeus's life's work – 14,000 plants, 3,198 insects, 1,564 shells, about 3,000 letters and 1,600 books – and, soon after, founded the Linnean Society. It is here that the collection now resides, intact, in its subterranean repository. Smith's purchase was a pivotal moment in botanical history for it provided the material for Britain to advance the Linnaean system of classification of the natural world.

There is an apocryphal tale that the Swedes realised too late that Linnaeus's herbarium and library were leaving their shores, and sent a gunboat to pursue the London-bound ship onto which they had been carefully packed, but there is no evidence for it. Certainly, Joseph Banks made no mention of it when he wrote to the Swedish botanist and taxonomist Olof Swartz in February 1788, telling him of the Linnean Society's foundation: 'a new Society was instituted here last Tuesday Chiefly under the Direction of Dr Smith who purchased Linnaeus's herbarium it is Calld the Linnaean Society & intended for the purpose of Publishing new species of Plants animals &c. I incline to think it will flourish as great care is taken in the institution to keep out improper people.'

In 1873, the Society moved into its present premises, a purpose-built wing of Burlington House. Today, in the meeting room, Linnaeus's portrait takes centre stage above an impressive oak dais that is carved with his signature flower, the tea-yielding twinflower (*Linnaea borealis*). The Dutch botanist Jan Gronovius named the plant after the great taxonomist who, while having a deep affection for it, described it self-deprecatingly as 'a plant of Lapland, lowly, insignificant and disregarded, flowering but for a brief space – from

Linnaeus who resembles it'. Linnaeus's advocacy of the plant as Lapp tea was less successful than that of plant naming; his botanist son later described the tea from the twinflower as 'rather repulsive'.

Joseph Banks, who had helped safeguard Linnaeus's collections, was one of the most remarkable gentleman scholars and men of affairs of the eighteenth century. The establishment of government-funded posts for professional scientists began only in the late nine-teenth century; before then, most scientists either held roles in the professions, or were independently wealthy. In the absence of a national museum of natural history, inherited wealth was needed to build up large personal collections and libraries; even once the British Museum had been founded by a legacy under the will of Hans Sloane in 1753, its biological collections were long poorly cared for.

Banks was the heir to the wealthy Revesby estate in Lincolnshire and, after his father's death in 1761, was fully able to fulfil his enthusiasm for botany. When, as a student at Oxford, he found the professor of botany reluctant to teach – indeed, he had deliv-ered only one lecture in thirty-five years – Banks arranged for a Cambridge botanist to deliver lectures instead. This early episode is indicative of Banks's ability to act decisively, spending as much money as required to achieve his aims.

In 1768, Banks funded himself and seven others, including Linnaeus's student Daniel Solander, to accompany James Cook on an expedition to observe the transit of the planet Venus and find the *Terra Australis Incognita*, the 'unknown southern land'. This mythical place was believed to exist to counterbalance land masses in the northern hemisphere. The naturalist John Ellis had kept the ageing Linnaeus abreast of the preparations, writing to him:

No people ever went to sea better fitted out for the purpose of Natural History, nor more elegantly. They have got a fine library of Natural History; they have all sorts of machines for catching and preserving insects; all kinds of nets, trawls, drags and hooks for coral fishing; they even have a curious contrivance of a telescope by which, put into the water, you can see the bottom to a great depth, where it is clear. They have many cases of bottles with ground stoppers of several sizes to preserve animals in spirits. They have the several sorts of salts to surround the seeds; and wax, both bees-wax and that of the *Myrica*. They have two painters and draughtsmen, several volunteers who have a tolerable notion of Natural History; in short, Solander assured me this expedition would cost Mr. Banks £10,000.

Although the expedition didn't venture as far south as Antarctica, it did reach the Antipodes. The *Endeavour* left Plymouth in August 1768, stopping first at Madeira and then Rio de Janeiro. It then

The *Endeavour* expedition on the coast of New Holland
(New South Wales, Australia), June 1770

sailed south for Tierra del Fuego, where on an ill-judged mission two of Banks's servants died of cold while plant-collecting in the snow. Exploration, which brought so many new plants to Europe at this time and did so much to stimulate interest in botany, was a dangerous business.

Christmas Day was spent at sea. Banks wrote in his journal: 'Christmas Day: all good Christians, that is to say, all good hands, got abominably drunk, so that all through the night there was scarce a sober man in the ship. Weather, thank God, very moderate, or the Lord knows what would have become of us.' From South America, the ship visited Tahiti and New Zealand, before landing on the fertile east coast of Australia in 1770. Cook named this New South Wales and claimed it for Britain. Banks persuaded Cook to name the bay on which they first landed 'Botany Bay' on account of its wealth of plants. After a few days immersed in studying and collecting this abundant flora, Banks wrote: 'Our collection of Plants was now grown so immensely [sic] large that it was necessary that some extraordinary care should be taken of them least they should spoil in the books [in which they were placed to be dried].'

Banks's journal also recorded the sailors' uneasy relationship with the Aborigines living around Botany Bay and his first encounter with a kangaroo, 'an animal as large as a greyhound, of a mouse colour, and very swift'. After leaving Botany Bay, the ship followed the coastline to the north. Banks noted the same plants that he'd encountered in the East Indies. Of the stretch of coast now called Moreton Bay, he wrote:

> We went ashore and found several plants which we had not before seen; among them, however, were still more East Indian plants than in the last harbour; one kind of grass which we had also seen there was very troublesome to us. Its sharp seeds were bearded

backwards, and whenever they stuck into our clothes were by these beards pushed forwards until they got into the flesh. This grass was so plentiful that it was scarcely possible to avoid it, and, with the mosquitos that were likewise innumerable, made walking almost intolerable.

The toil and discomfort were worth it, however. Using Linnaeus's brand-new grammar of plant classification, Banks and his assistant Daniel Solander managed to amass and identify 3,600 species on board the *Endeavour*, 1,400 of which were new to science. Banks was presented to King George III and became something of a celebrity. The acclaimed cartoon of Banks as a 'botanic macaroni' dates to 1772, just after his return. A 'macaroni' was a foppish graduate of the Grand Tour, and here it refers both to Banks's extensive travels and to the common perception that here was an ambitious social climber rather than a serious man of science.

Banks had planned to accompany Captain Cook on a second voyage but his request for fifteen personal members of staff, including two French horn players, was not received kindly. When Cook pointed out that the modifications required to accommodate Banks's men would make the ship top heavy, Banks withdrew from the expedition. Wishing to employ his team 'in some way or other to the advancement of Science', he made a voyage to Iceland instead. However, this was not a great success: it being late in the season, there were few plants available to collect. Thereafter Banks divided his time between his house in London and his family estate in Lincolnshire.

By the early 1780s, he was enjoying life as a Baronet, the President of the Royal Society, an advisor to cabinet ministers and a patron of the sciences on a global scale, in addition to operating a 'kind of superintendence over his [the King's] Royal Botanic Gardens'.

His friendship with the King grew steadily, thanks to their shared interest in rural affairs. Banks was convinced that Britain was destined to be the major civilising power in the world and could achieve this by harnessing science – particularly botany – and imperial progress together, to their mutual benefit.

His role at Kew was not always limited to the botanical. When 'Farmer George' wanted to improve the quality of British wool, Banks helped smuggle Spanish merino sheep across Portugal and then on to Kew, where they grazed around the Pagoda. Some were eventually auctioned off and made their way to New South Wales, where they helped to found Australia's merino wool industry. By 1820, Australia was farming 33,818 sheep.

Banks's interests encompassed agricultural improvement, political power and science. Like Linnaeus, he wanted to use plants and botany to help his nation to become self-sufficient. However,

Eighteenth-century engraving of sheep at Kew,
after William Woollett

Banks was more outward looking than the Swede. Whereas Linnaeus had sought to reduce his country's reliance on imports by cultivating newly discovered tropical plants on Swedish soil, Banks had a wider vision of improving the world and proposed to do so by 'enclosing' common land. At the time, large parts of Britain were commonly owned; anyone, no matter how poor, could graze animals, pick fruits or gather firewood on these 'commons'. Banks viewed these areas as derelict terrain that might help feed the rising population. He therefore supported the Enclosure Acts, which turned common land into private property that would be cultivated and maintained. As Jim Endersby explains, 'This is very much how Banks sees the world, as a series of waste grounds or common lands that are waiting to be enclosed, waiting to be improved.'

Banks put Kew at the heart of his vision to make the world's wastelands productive. Starting with Francis Masson, the plant hunter who had collected Kew's prized *Encephalartos altensteinii*, he despatched plant collectors across the globe to bring back all kinds of new and potentially useful species. Writing to Archibald Menzies, who travelled as a naturalist and surgeon on HMS *Discovery* on a round-the-world voyage between 1791 and 1794, Banks was specific in his requirements:

When you meet with curious or valuable plants which you do not think likely to be propagated from seeds in His Majesties Garden, you are to dig up proper specimens of them, plant them in the glass Frame provided for that purpose, and use your utmost endeavours to preserve them alive till your return, and you are to consider every one of them, as well as all Seeds of Plants which you shall collect during the voyage, as wholly and entirely the property of His Majesty, and on no account whatever to part with any of them, or any cuttings, Slips, or parts of them, for any purpose whatever but for His Majesty's use.

At Banks's instigation, the young plant hunter William Kerr went to China, gathering tiger lilies and the double yellow Banksian rose. Meanwhile, Kew gardeners Allan Cunningham and James Bowie collected in Brazil before setting sail for New South Wales and South Africa respectively.

In 1792, Banks boasted proudly of the fruits of his collectors' labours to one of his naturalist contemporaries.

Kew Gardens proceeds with increased vigor [sic]. The additions of plants lately receivd [sic] are indeed very interesting. We have 3 Magnolias from China, one only of which was before known among us and that only from Kaempfer's *Icones* [a botanical publication that Banks published] . . . Epidendrums blossom away daily; *E. vanilla* is as high as the glass & will soon produce flowers. Ferns are propagated from seed of the West Indies so that the Garden must soon overflow.

Although Banks never again travelled abroad himself, in effect he brought the world to his London home at 32 Soho Square, turning it into a well-organised academy of natural history. By initiating expeditions that would bring back information about native peoples and their customs, along with botanical and zoological specimens, he was able to build up a virtual picture of foreign lands, knowledge that informed new expeditions. He also put his own experiences of New South Wales to good use, advising the government prior to a voyage there by the *Investigator*. It was Banks who named the ship, gave the captain Matthew Flinders detailed instructions on what to do and where to go, and secured the services of Scottish botanist Robert Brown for the trip. In effect, he made the *Investigator* into a telescope, through which he could observe faraway continents. Without going back to Australia, he was able to make Australia come to him in the form of maps, specimens and accounts of voyages.

Having been among the first Europeans to set foot in Botany Bay, Banks also advised the government that the location might be a suitable spot on which to found a penal colony provided European crops and livestock were introduced. In his journal from the voyage on *Endeavour*, he had observed that the woods were 'free from under wood of every kind and the trees [were] at such a distance from one another that the whole Country or at least a great part of it might be cultivated without being oblig'd to cut down a single tree'. When the government took up Banks's advice, he then helped compile a 'portmanteau collection of plants' comprising European vegetables, herbs, berries, fruits and grains that he thought suitable for the local conditions.

A contemporary description of the embryonic nation, written by settler and author James Atkinson, suggests he chose well: 'The esculent [edible] and culinary vegetables and roots of Europe are all grown in great perfection, together with many others that cannot be raised in England without the aid of artificial heat. Fruits are in great abundance and variety, and many of excellent quality.'

Beyond Australia, Banks was instrumental in helping settlers establish botanical gardens in India, Ceylon (Sri Lanka), St Vincent, Trinidad and Jamaica, often employing his trusted plant collectors to run the gardens. His desire was that valuable plants from one colony would be shipped to sister gardens in other locations, where they could be grown profitably. He hoped, through this network of botanical gardens, to realise his dream of 'improvement'. In

Botanical Garden, St Vincent, one of the oldest colonial gardens, founded 1765

reality, communication difficulties made achieving this impossible in his lifetime. A letter sent to Australia, for example, could take several months to get there, making it hard for Banks to give instructions or receive feedback. In one case, the intended recipient of a letter addressed to the botanical garden in Sydney was dead by the time it arrived. As a result, Banks – and Kew – had a very limited degree of control over Britain's burgeoning botanical empire.

When Banks and King George III both died in 1820, Kew lost its botanical leader and its royal supporter at once. It also lost the collective intelligence of Banks's library and herbarium specimens, which, unlike Linnaeus's books and manuscripts, became separated. Robert Brown, who had become Banks's librarian, inherited the books and herbarium specimens for the duration of his lifetime; on his death they were to go to the British Museum but, in the event, he agreed to the transfer in 1827. Banks's papers, meanwhile, went to his wife's relative, Lord Brabourne, whose offer to sell them to the Museum in 1880 for £250 was refused. As a result they were put on the open market and became dispersed, like wind-blown seeds, around the world.

While Banks had helped to ensure that Linnaeus's classification lived on after he died, his own legacy was in danger of withering away. It would take other visionaries to realise, for Britain, the riches represented by the world's diverse flora.

3

PRESSED PLANTS
AND POSSIBILITIES

Herbarium sheet of *Poa ligularis*, collected by Charles Darwin,
with his signature

I N A GLASS-SIDED meeting room at Kew, a group of botanists eagerly inspect a stack of pages from the Nigerian newspaper the *Sun*. They are not interested in the African fashionistas who smile out from the pages, however, but in the dried specimens of twigs, leaves and flowers that lie, flattened, between each folded sheet. Taxonomists from Kew's Wet Tropics (Africa) team had collected the specimens with UK and local colleagues in Gashaka Gumti National Park, Nigeria, and brought them back to West London. They could include rare or unknown species, or yield an important medicinal drug, but until they are correctly identified no one can know. Finding out more about this park's flora is critical, because 90 per cent of its forest has already been lost. Today's meeting, to sort the specimens into their respective plant families, is the first step towards unravelling their mysteries. Once this has been accomplished, each plant will be despatched to the relevant taxonomist for identification to species level, mounted on acid-free paper and then filed in its scientifically correct place among the 7.5 million specimens that make up the great dried-plant 'family tree' of Kew's Herbarium.

A herbarium is a collection of plant specimens that have been pressed, dried and either attached to a sheet of paper or preserved in spirit in glass jars. The presence of a herbarium is one of the characteristics that sets a botanical garden apart from any other kind.

The earliest herbaria, known as 'horti sicci' (dry gardens), were formed in Italy's new physic gardens of the sixteenth century and were made up of sheets of paper bearing dried plants, bound into books. This was how Hans Sloane kept his magnificent collection of botanical specimens, left to the British Museum in 1753. However, during the eighteenth century the arrival of an abundance of new species – the spoil of voyages of exploration – in tandem with the new tool of Linnaean classification, made it more convenient for loose sheets to be used, which could be reordered as new species or new classifications arose. This was the form taken by Joseph Banks's herbarium.

One of the characteristics that distinguishes a herbarium from a library or museum store is that, in a well-curated herbarium, the order in which specimens are stored will be rearranged from time to time in order to reflect a new understanding of plant relationships. A herbarium that is static would simply be a museum of dead plants; instead, a herbarium is a living research tool.

In Kew's Herbarium, one of the largest in the world, each sheet displays a sample of an individual specimen. Species from the same genus (the taxonomic grouping below that of family) are filed together in a folder; folders containing plants from different genera are then placed together in a cupboard that includes a particular family. The job of Kew's taxonomists, drawing on their expertise in global plant diversity, is to ensure that each species is filed in its correct place, alongside its closest relatives. That way, scientists wanting to learn about a particular plant's attributes will know where to locate the relevant specimen. The Herbarium's specimens, which have come from all over the world and were collected by an extraordinary range of people over hundreds of years, form a crucial reference library for the work of Kew. As Keeper of the Herbarium Dave Simpson explains: 'The oldest specimen that we have goes back to 1700 but the majority came to us in the mid-nineteenth century.'

Old specimens, such as those from Joseph Banks's herbarium that are now at Kew, differ chiefly from modern ones in the quality of the labelling. A modern label will be a mine of information, including the location from where the plant was collected and the ecology of its surroundings. It will also contain details of the plant that are not obvious from the specimen, such as tree height or original flower colour. In contrast, an old specimen may simply bear the year or country of collection, if that.

Kew's Herbarium itself dates back to 1840, when the Gardens' ownership passed from the royal family to the government. By the 1830s, thanks to Joseph Banks, many of Britain's colonies had botanical gardens but they had been set up in a somewhat ad hoc fashion. Some had come about because of a local governor's passion for botany, whereas others had been founded simply to provide work for convicts. In 1838, John Lindley – Professor of Botany at University College London, and Assistant Secretary of the Horticultural Society of London – wrote a report for the government on the various royal gardens, which had been in decline since the deaths of both George III and Banks in 1820. The Treasury had raised the question of whether all the royal gardens were really required, with an eye to saving costs.

Instead of closure, Lindley proposed Kew's transfer from royal patronage to government funding 'for the promotion of Botanical Science throughout the Empire'. He believed that, if centrally managed by Kew, Britain's motley collection of colonial gardens overseas could greatly benefit medicine, commerce, agriculture and horticulture: 'They should all be under the control of the chief of the garden, acting in concert with him, and through him with each other, reporting constantly [on] their proceedings, explaining their wants, receiving their supplies, and aiding the mother country in everything that is useful in the vegetable kingdom.'

For the government to investigate the commercial wealth of its disparate botanical resources, it needed Kew to establish what plants there were and where they grew. Lindley – who had worked at Banks's London house, using his collections to help classify roses – addressed this in the report, calling for 'an extensive herbarium and considerable library' to assist in the identification and naming of plants. William Jackson Hooker, the man chosen by the government to develop Kew as a national botanic garden, took Lindley's report to heart. A keen collector and classifier of plants, he had identified his first species new to Britain, the moss *Buxbaumia aphylla*, at the age of twenty. When he arrived to take up the post of Director at Kew in 1841, he brought with him his own herbarium and library, which took up several rooms of his residence, West Park. He was ambitious in his aims: 'I regard not any reasonable expense and am determined as far as lies in my power to make my Herbarium the richest of any private one in Europe.'

Over time, Hooker encouraged other botanists and organisations to part with their collections to form a separate herbarium for Kew. The herbarium of the botanist and traveller William Bromfeld was the first official acquisition in 1852; two years later, four large railway wagons of specimens arrived from the botanist George Bentham; and in 1858 several large collections, partly destroyed by vermin and damp, were donated by the East India Company.

Many plants that found their way into Kew's Herbarium were sent to Hooker by individual botanists. During the early nineteenth century, correspondence between poorly paid, part-time naturalists and wealthy scientific gentlemen was common. Part-timers – who often could neither afford expensive natural history monographs nor gain entry to the relevant museums, both being essential for classifying specimens – sought to befriend 'gentlemen' collectors who had access to these resources. In this way they gleaned knowledge on their chosen subject in exchange for the specimens they collected in their local areas. They also gained a certain status from possessing the knowledge and skills to match those of the gentlemen collectors.

In the course of his lifetime, Hooker, keen to share the thrill of discovery with others, encouraged many botanists to correspond with him. He crossed rigid social divides in the pursuit of scientific truth, for many of the collectors he mentored were working-class artisans, frequently devoting themselves to studying diminutive plants such as mosses and lichens, which, like them, lived below the social radar. These keen botanisers scoured their localities, looking for unusual plants, consulting Hooker, deferentially, when they couldn't place a particular specimen. William Bentley, a blacksmith from Royton, near Manchester, wrote tentatively: 'It is with some little diffidence that I approach you through the medium of this paper . . . but we tiny labourers in the extensive field of botany have no one else upon whom to look, [and] we consider you as the father of the science to whom must be submitted all our difficulties.'

Hooker's network of correspondents extended far beyond his native shores. Several keen naturalists wrote to him from Van Diemen's Land (now Tasmania), off the coast of Australia, which had been colonised and set up as a penal colony in 1803. The island's lush temperate rainforests yielded rich pickings of novel botanical specimens in the early decades of the nineteenth century.

Engraving of Kew's first Museum of Economic Botany,
opened in 1847

Ronald Campbell Gunn, a superintendent of convicts and a prolific plant collector, admitted his difficulties in identifying and naming plants in a letter to Hooker dated 21 April 1838:

> I am now becoming anxious to know the new or undescribed from the well known plants – it would enable me to discriminate in Collecting, and of many I am even still ignorant of the Genera – Backhouse [James Backhouse, a naturalist who visited Australia's convict colonies] used to say – Better give a plant a wrong name than none at all, but I am not inclined to follow that principle as I find erroneous names once given most pertinaciously adhere – whereas a plant without a name is ready to receive the true one.

Between 1832 and 1860, Gunn sent many hundreds of specimens to Hooker, requesting in exchange primarily reference works to help improve his own knowledge: 'You cannot err in sending me Books upon any subject – Botanical Medical, &c, &c. For the latter my botany has given me a strong taste.'

Over the years, as Hooker's loyal correspondents sent specimens by the caseload, his own herbarium swelled. In 1853, the collection moved, with Hooker, from West Park to Hunter House, a detached house beside the Thames formerly inhabited by the King of Hanover. After Hooker's death in 1865, the government bought his personal herbarium for £1,000, merging it with Kew's collection. In 1877, a wing was built on Hunter House to accommodate it but space continued to be a problem. As William Thiselton-Dyer, Director of Kew at the time, explained to the Office of Works in 1899: 'I cannot control the expansion of Kew Herbarium because I cannot control the expansion of the Empire. The scientific investigation of new territories follows their accretion.' Three more wings had to be added to the building between 1902 and 1968, with further expansion into the quadrangle in 1988.

In 2007, with specimens still arriving at a rate of between 35,000 and 50,000 per year, Kew commissioned the firm of Edward Cullinan Architects to build a climate-controlled extension, measuring 5,000 square metres, to house part of the Herbarium and the library. Designed to keep floodwaters and pests at bay, it should provide sufficient room to house the collection for another fifty years.

Today, strict rules dictate how arriving specimens make their way from the curved timber and glass lobby of the new building to their rightful place within the Herbarium's extensive botanical filing system. Initially stored on purpose-built black shelves, any parcels containing plant material make a right turn through double doors into Kew's 'Dirty Area'. Here, for three days, they are frozen in large walk-in freezers at a temperature of minus 40°C, to kill any plant-devouring pests, such as the beetle *Trogoderma angustum,* and their eggs. Only then can they be taken to the adjoining Collections Management Unit (CMU) and opened up. Every specimen consignment that comes in is given a unique number, so it can be tracked on its path through the Herbarium. Coloured tags identify whether parcels are incoming loans, outgoing loans or gifts, or specimens to be identified and placed in the Herbarium.

It can take newly arrived specimens up to a year to be filed correctly within the Herbarium and once they arrive in a particular folder, they might not stay there for long. As new information emerges about plants' relationships with one another, so their positions in the Herbarium shift to reflect these findings. Recent advances in DNA technology, in particular, have prompted some major reorganisation. In 1869, the specimens in the Herbarium were arranged according to a classification system devised by

Kew Herbarium, inspecting and identifying
newly arrived plant specimens

William Hooker's son, Joseph, and the botanist George Bentham. This system reflected contemporary views on the evolutionary relationships of plants, which had changed considerably since Linnaeus's day. In recent years, there have been significant further advances in our knowledge about how plants are related to each other, thanks to studies using molecular characteristics and DNA gene sequencing (see Chapter 21).

Kew's Herbarium is now being arranged according to this new system, known as APG III (APG stands for Angiosperm Phylogeny Group, which is an informal network of botanists, formed in the mid-1990s with the purpose of using the results of DNA sequencing to produce a new family classification for the angiosperms, or flowering plants). The shift has thrown up some surprising new relationships. For example, the corpse flower (*Rafflesia*), which grows in tropical Asia and has the largest individual flower of all plants – it reaches one metre across and smells of rotting flesh – is related to the poinsettia (*Euphorbia pulcherrima*), which has one of the world's smallest flowers. The red 'petals' of the latter are, in fact, bracts surrounding the flowers.

The organic way in which Kew's Herbarium has grown and altered over the years becomes apparent on a tour around it. The new building, with its floor-to-ceiling windows, in every way befits the high-tech tools and techniques employed by modern taxonomists. Meanwhile the oldest wing of the Herbarium, with its ornate red spiral staircases, high ceilings and wooden parquet flooring, still recalls the days of Empire when much of the world's flora was largely unknown.

Individual specimen sheets also reflect Kew's long heritage. In one of the Herbarium's folders are three dried stalks of the perennial grass *Poa ligularis*, at least one of which was collected by Charles Darwin on his voyage to Patagonia on the *Beagle* between 1831 and 1836. The plants, their tangled corn-coloured leaves firmly glued to the sheet, are topped by full seed heads. Darwin annotated the sheet by hand, locating his collection: 'Bahia Blanca, Coast of Patagonia, early in Oct 1832, C. Darwin.' The sheet, on the signature blue paper of William Hooker's Herbarium, is stamped 'Herbarium Hookerianum 1867', the date when the collection officially came under Kew's ownership.

Later additions are a Kew barcode, showing that the sheet has been digitised to enable its examination by botanists online anywhere in the world. As Assistant Keeper Bill Baker explains: 'Darwin's original specimen is still very usable; you can still detach a floret and boil it up [to rehydrate it for examination]. It's important not to see these dried plants just as historical artefacts. This is one of Kew's 350,000 "Type" specimens [the original specimens on which new species descriptions have been based]. Types typify and fix species names for all time. While not necessarily scientifically important, they are the way we curate and manage names.'

It was a love of order and hierarchy that compelled the Victorians to begin building up Kew's Herbarium 150 years ago. Their own world was regulated into, as they saw it, a divinely sanctioned system of aristocrats, merchants and labourers, of Britain and her colonies, of Christians and heathens. They recognised that plants had the same sense of order, and the Herbarium was seen as a physical manifestation of that hierarchy.

As new additions have arrived down the years, Kew's Herbarium has grown to become much greater than the sum of its meticulously filed parts. Its organisation, based on plant relationships, has enabled botanists to make connections that would never otherwise have been found. For example, in the late 1980s, scientists were seeking new anti-viral drugs with which to treat HIV. They had found a promising chemical in *Castanospermum australe*, a tree that was endemic to eastern Australia but only in small populations. When the scientists approached Kew to see whether it might have a close relative that would yield the same or a similar drug, the Gardens' taxonomists pinpointed a more widely available South American species that turned out to contain exactly the same chemical. Without the Herbarium resource, it is unlikely anyone would ever have looked in South America.

The Herbarium is also proving useful in the face of changing global climates, since each specimen carries a range of botanical information about the plant and the locations from which it was collected. In modern collections, this includes highly accurate location data gathered using global positioning systems. With shifts

Interior of the Kew Herbarium which houses 7.5 million
dried plant specimens

in climate affecting the life cycles of plants, this array of data is invaluable for identifying distribution changes in plant habitats. As Baker explains: 'The key thing is that the Herbarium records what plants have occurred where, allowing us to see whether their distribution has changed over time, shrinking perhaps with habitat destruction. In this way we can quantify the extinction threat faced by species.'

Back in the meeting to sort specimens into families, Martin Cheek, who heads the Wet Tropics (Africa) team, works methodically to identify a dried specimen with tendrils coiling from its stem. This feature limits the plant to three families: Cucurbitaceae (cucumbers), Vitaceae (grapevines) or Passifloraceae (passion flowers). He judges it to belong to the cucumber family, by looking at details of the tendrils' position and the fruit. This time-consuming work, which requires considerable experience, is crucial for conserving Africa's diverse flora. Similar collections made in neighbouring Cameroon between 1995 and 2003 yielded 2,440 plant species, a tenth of which were new to science.

These specimens, combined with studies of those in the Herbarium dating back to William Hooker's day, enabled Kew's scientists to identify 815 of the 2,440 species as 'threatened' under the assessment criteria drawn up by the International Union for Conservation of Nature. Kew's maps showed that areas containing high densities of threatened species did not tally well with the footprint of existing national parks, which had been set up with animals, rather than plants, in mind. As a result, the government of Cameroon created the 29,320-hectare Bakossi National Park to protect the new-found biodiversity hotspot. As Cheek explains: 'Before we started our work, this area in Cameroon wasn't on any conservation map. By the time we finished, it ranked as one of the top two documented centres for plant diversity in tropical Africa.'

Born of a Victorian passion for collecting, Kew's Herbarium has become a vital tool for conserving the world's flora.

4

BLIGHT ON THE LANDSCAPE

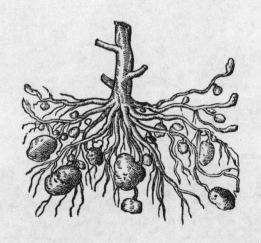

Irish peasant girl guarding the family's last
few possessions, 1886

I N THE FIRST half of the nineteenth century, Ireland's population almost doubled, from 4.5 million in 1800 to more than 8 million in 1845. Feeding such huge numbers was made possible primarily because Irish peasant farmers had adopted the potato as their main crop. A vegetable native to South America, it had first been introduced to Europe by Spanish conquistadors in the sixteenth century and then became widely distributed. Because this humble tuber provided protein, carbohydrates, vitamins and minerals, it was possible for people to live off little else, and many poor Irish farmers did just that. However, relying solely on the potato for sustenance was to be their downfall.

In the early summer of 1845, Ireland's potato crop was thriving in the sunny weather. Yet when the sunshine gave way to endless days of rain, the potatoes began rotting in their sodden beds. First, black or brown lesions developed on the tops of the leaves; then, white halos of mildew appeared on their undersides. The leaves soon withered into a stinking compost and the potatoes themselves followed suit, rotting in the ground or in the store. The disease infected 40 per cent of the country's crop. Irish peasants watched helplessly when the following year it struck again, this time emerging earlier in the season. Although the Irish had planted some grain crops, these were needed to pay rent to their English landlords. With no food to sustain the population, more than a million people starved to death and another million were driven to emigrate.

The English novelist Anthony Trollope, then in his early thirties, summed up the horror in his novel *Castle Richmond*:

> They who were in the south of Ireland during the winter of 1846–47 will not readily forget the agony of that period. For many, many years preceding and up to that time, the increasing swarms of the country had been fed upon the potato, and upon the potato only; and now all at once the potato failed them, and the greater part of eight million human beings were left without food. The destruction of the potato was the work of God; and it was natural to attribute the sufferings which at once overwhelmed the unfortunate country to God's anger – to his wrath for the misdeeds of which that country had been guilty. For myself, I do not believe in such exhibitions of God's anger.

We now know that the disease was caused, not by religious decree, but by *Phytophthora infestans*, a water mould. Water moulds resemble fungi and can be parasitic (feeding on living tissue) or saprotrophic (feeding on dead tissue). *P. infestans* was first described in 1845 by Camille Montagne, a French physician in Napoleon's army. He shared his findings with Miles Joseph Berkeley, a British clergyman and authority on fungi. Berkeley was the first scientist to recognise that the organism (which he believed to be a fungus) was the cause of the blight, writing in the *Journal of the Horticultural Society of London* in 1846: 'The decay is the consequence of the presence of the mould, and not the mould of the decay. It is not the habit of the allied species to prey on decayed or decaying matter, but to produce decay – a fact which is of the first importance.'

Today, Berkeley's extensive collection of fungus samples forms the foundation of Kew's Fungarium. Within the many green boxes containing around 1.25 million specimens are some of the original specimens of potato blight from Montagne that Berkeley used in his research. On a sheet displaying three dried potato leaves, mottled with late blight, are the detailed pencil drawings Berkeley made as he examined the mould under a microscope, trying to fathom out the relationship between it and the disease. (These drawings were reproduced in his 1846 article.)

Bryn Dentinger, Head of Mycology at Kew, explains:

Most water moulds grow filamentously in their [unseen] vegetative phase. They will reproduce asexually with spores that swim in liquid under optimal conditions, such as high humidity and warm temperatures, enabling them to rapidly increase their numbers and outcompete other organisms.

'Although it is rare in *P. infestans*, if compatible mates are present they will at some point go into a sexual phase. This usually happens when conditions are no longer conducive to growth: if it's cold, or they've run out of food, or it's dry. In these circumstances they will produce thick-walled, dark-coloured, resting spores that can survive for several years in the soil while they wait for the conditions to again become conducive to growth. At that point, they will germinate and produce a tube that will either start making spores right away, or branch out and eventually become a tangled, interwoven, filamentous structure.

By examining the form of the 'fungus' under the microscope, Berkeley was able to draw the conclusion that the culprit was potato blight. Not everyone agreed with him, however. John Lindley, Professor of Botany at University College London, who had saved

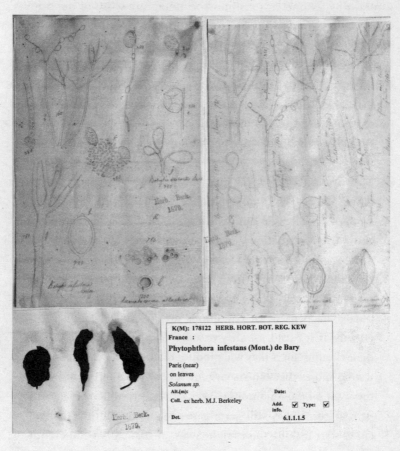

Blighted potato leaves and original sketches by Miles Joseph Berkeley
of *Phytophthora infestans*

Kew for the nation, was convinced that it was decay, due to wet conditions, that had caused the fungus and not the other way round. The two of them hotly debated the topic through the pages of the *Gardeners' Chronicle*.

Eventually, in 1861, Berkeley was proved right by the German surgeon and mycologist Anton de Bary. De Bary grew potato plants in the cool, wet environmental conditions that favoured blight. He applied the white sporangia (cases containing spores) from diseased potatoes to some plants, while keeping others as 'control' plants with no fungus. Only the plants de Bary infected with the pathogen succumbed to the disease, despite the wet conditions. It was clear that the plants did not rot away because they had absorbed too much water, as Lindley and his followers had thought.

Today, de Bary is considered the founding father of plant pathology. 'What he brought to the field of mycology that hadn't been there before was an obsession with understanding the development of organisms,' explains Dentinger. 'It was really his meticulous, tedious study of life cycles, and the structure that makes up those life cycles, that allowed him to propose, convincingly, to the rest of the world that the fungus associated with late blight of potatoes was the cause of the disease.'

Resolving this fundamental question was of major significance. It triggered advances in the study of plant, human and animal diseases by making scientists aware of how contaminated food and water, and unsterilised medical instruments, could help spread contagious diseases. This understanding prompted scientists to abandon the idea that disease was the product of 'spontaneous generation', encouraging them instead to embrace Louis Pasteur's 'germ theory', first proposed in 1863, that some diseases were caused by micro-organisms. Although people had observed disease-causing organisms for 200 years, previously they had considered that the organisms resulted from the disease, rather than being the cause of it. And from the tragedy of the potato famine grew a new perspective on the natural world. Disease was no longer a dark and magical force but a biological activity, involving tiny parasites that invaded the plants and caused them to decay.

Providing answers raised new questions, however. At the time, scientists did not know what the tiny but lethal spores were that had caused havoc in the potato crop in Ireland. They knew not whether fungi were plants or animals; they had no idea where they disappeared to when they were not fruiting; and their method of reproduction remained a complete mystery. One of the late nineteenth-century scientists who sought to investigate the varying roles of fungi was Beatrix Potter, now far better known for her illustrated children's books. Her illustrations of fungi were very detailed and accurate, and she ventured into professional mycology. For example, she painted not only the fruiting bodies, but all other parts, at all ages, in the fungus life cycle and experimented with germinating the reproductive spores. And she drew the first record in Britain of the fungus *Tremella simplex*.

As a result of her meticulous observations of the fungi and their habits, Potter became fascinated by lichens. These organisms, which inhabit some of the most extreme environments on earth, were a puzzle to scientists in the nineteenth century. A Swiss scientist, Simon Schwendener, supported an idea first proposed by de Bary that they were formed of two different creatures, a fungus and algae, living together in a type of parasitic relationship. From her observations, Potter became convinced that Schwendener was right. However, like most women in science at that time, she found it difficult to be taken seriously. Jim Endersby takes up the story. 'In 1874, the British naturalist James

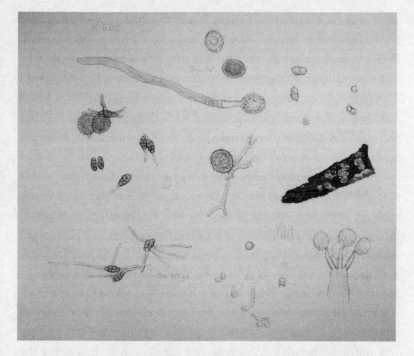

Illustration by Beatrix Potter of fungus *Aleurodiscus amorphus*
and spores of three other fungi, including *Tremella simplex*, 1896

Crombie, ridiculed the whole idea of the lichen being an unnatural union between a "captive algal damsel" and a "tyrant fungal master". The fact that Beatrix Potter had attached her name to this rather outlandish theory didn't help her get a fair hearing for her ideas.'

In Potter's zeal to find out the truth about lichens, she cultivated algal cells and fungal spores in her kitchen, to observe how the two partners joined together to form one organism. The best place to present the findings of such studies was the Linnean Society, but at the time women were not admitted as members. When her work was finally presented there in 1897, it had to be read on her behalf by George Massee, Kew's mycologist. In her private journal, Potter expressed her disdain for her ambassador: 'I opine that he had passed several stages of development into a fungus himself.' The peer-reviewed paper needed further revisions but Potter never finalised it. Apparently disillusioned with the scientific world after this experience, she concentrated on writing and illustrating her fantasies for children instead.

The idea that there might be a link between fungi and plants was given further credence by the work of Albert Bernhard Frank who, in 1881, was commissioned by the German government to find a way to increase the harvest of truffles, a prized edible fungus. Although he was unsuccessful, he noted that the roots of the oak and beech trees where truffles grew were always covered in fungi. He observed that the fungi did not appear to cause damage; rather, the trees in question were healthy and vigorous. Frank published a paper in which he put forward the theory that this relationship was mutually beneficial to plant and fungus. In it, he coined the term mycorrhiza, meaning 'fungus root'. We now know that mycorrhizal fungi form a mutualistic relationship with the plant, colonising the roots and sending out extremely fine filaments into the soil, which act as root extensions.

'There are large multitudes of fungi but only limited numbers of roots available, which leads to very high levels of colonisation,' says Martin Bidartondo, Senior Lecturer in Biology at Imperial College London and Honorary Research Associate at Kew, who studies the ecology and life cycles of these remarkable fungi. 'Most roots have mycorrhizal fungi growing in them which are able to grow out from the plant and produce more spores. They might do this by producing mushrooms, which we are all familiar with; or by turning into truffles; or by simply sending out spores into the soil. In this way they restart the cycle, getting out into the environment to find new plants. Fungi affect the growth of different plants in various ways. Biologists are very interested in what creates diversity – both of plant responses and of species in ecosystems. Mycorrhizae seem to have considerable impact on how that occurs.'

There is still much to learn in the field of mycology. Recent analyses of DNA in soils have suggested there are between 5 and 6 million species of fungi worldwide but, at present, we have a detailed understanding of less than 5 per cent. Genetic sequencing is helping to fill in gaps in our knowledge; in particular it has revolutionised the classification of fungi, which, as with plants, was initially driven by their characteristic shapes, so those that resembled each other were considered to be related. We now know that many of those proposed relationships were wrong. For example, algae are not descended from a single common ancestor.

It was genetic sequencing, too, that in the 1990s helped mycologists to confirm that *Phytophthora infestans* is a stramenopile (a group of algae including water moulds and kelp), rather than a true fungus. New technology has allowed them to study whole genomes, comparing historical and contemporary specimens, and see essential differences. This has led to some surprising results. As Dentinger says: 'It was thought for a long time that the organism that caused the late blight of potato in the nineteenth century, wreaking such havoc in Ireland and beyond, was similar or identical to the strain that's causing blight today in our potato fields. But genome comparisons have revealed that it was a unique strain that existed for only about fifty years.'

5

LUMPING AND
SPLITTING

CURTIS'S
BOTANICAL MAGAZINE,

COMPRISING THE

Plants of the Royal Gardens of Kew

AND

OF OTHER BOTANICAL ESTABLISHMENTS IN GREAT BRITAIN;
WITH SUITABLE DESCRIPTIONS;

BY

JOSEPH DALTON HOOKER, M.D., F.R.S. L.S. & G.S.,

D.C.L. OXON., LL.D. CANTAB., CORRESPONDENT OF THE INSTITUTE OF FRANCE.

VOL. XXII.

OF THE THIRD SERIES;

(Or Vol. XCII. of the Whole Work.)

" In order, eastern flowers large,
Some drooping low their crimson bells
Half closed, and others studded wide
With disks and tiars, fed the time
With odour."

Tennyson.

LONDON:
L. REEVE & CO., 5, HENRIETTA STREET, COVENT GARDEN.
1866.

The world's oldest continuously published colour-illustrated
periodical, *Curtis's Botanical Magazine*, still produced by Kew

THE WEEKLY SOUTH-EAST Asia team 'sort' is under way at the Kew Herbarium, its purpose being both to identify incoming specimens and to be a forum for learning, as the family of each specimen is discussed. Today the plants under consideration by the group are from Papua New Guinea. The specimens, still wrapped in the *Sydney Morning Herald* and other Australian newspapers, have been sent to Kew by Harvard University's Herbarium, for confirmation of their identifications as well as to share their botanical riches.

This team – which solves botanical identification problems, tracks the location of familiar species and, sometimes, identifies new ones – is headed by one of Kew's expert taxonomists, Tim Utteridge. As he explains, holding up one rarity, 'Hardly anyone has previously recorded this. At maturity, it splits open, and inside are hundreds of seeds in this white, pulp-like marshmallow. We wondered whether it was a new species.' The questions go back and forth, as the scientists debate.

The discovery of new species is an essential part of Kew's scientific remit. It is also a huge responsibility and often a logistical challenge. Gwilym Lewis, Head of Legumes, explains: 'On my first ever expedition, to Borneo, back in the 1980s, I'd been trained up well enough to understand that, when I was up to my neck in a swamp, with my glasses sliding off my nose, sweat pouring down, mosquitoes biting me, the plant I had in my hand was indeed new to science. Knowing that it was new to science, and that it didn't have a scientific name, was a real buzz for me. And that's certainly what's kept me going for the last thirty years.'

'Names are a very integral part of what we do in a science context,' explains Mark Chase, Keeper of Kew's Jodrell Laboratory, named after T.J. Phillips Jodrell, who funded the first building in 1877. This is because one of the greatest questions in biology remains: what is a species? And how do we know where a species begins and ends?

By the mid-nineteenth century, identifying and classifying plants was seen as far more important than mere list making. Beyond those identifications, though, there were deeper issues: the naming of species was a matter of enormous dispute. Ferocious debates took place about how species originally came into existence. The concept of evolution, or the 'transmutation of species', was seen as controversial, radical and beyond the pale: a theory only for the upstart working classes intent on social revolution, not a fit study for England's drawing rooms. But a few thought otherwise. Charles Darwin had become increasingly convinced, during his long voyage around the world in the *Beagle*, from 1831 to 1836, that species could, and did, evolve. To prove evolution had taken place, he had to show that species actually changed, from one into another, by slow transmutation. To do this, he needed to enlist the help of his closest scientific friend, Joseph Hooker.

Born in 1817, Joseph was the younger son of William Jackson Hooker, the first official Director of Kew (discussed in Chapter 3). Joseph had spent his childhood listening eagerly to his father's lectures and practising botany with him. He longed to travel, and later in

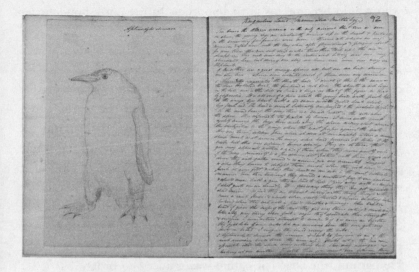

Pages from Joseph Hooker's *Antarctic Journal*,
May 1839–March 1843

life recalled: 'When still a child, I was very fond of Cook's *Voyages and Travels*; and my great delight was to sit on my grandfather's knee and look at the pictures . . . The one that took my fancy most was the plate of Christmas Harbour, Kerguelen Land, with the arched rock standing out to sea, and the sailors killing penguins; and I thought I should be the happiest boy alive if ever I would see that wonderful arched rock, and knock penguins on the head.'

Eventually, in 1839, aged twenty-two, Joseph Hooker accepted a medical post on board a Royal Navy ship, the HM *Erebus*, under Captain Ross, sailing to the southern oceans. Hooker hoped to follow in Darwin's illustrious footsteps, collecting specimens and producing research that he could publish back home in England. He also made important future contacts such as the missionary and printer William Colenso, whom he met in New Zealand and

61

who would become his most important future correspondent for the flora of those islands.

Hooker returned with many ideas about natural history, as well as large quantities of specimens, which were added to the Kew collection. He continued to collect, using his father's extensive list of contacts among botanical enthusiasts across the world. Once Hooker finally took up a position at Kew alongside his father, it gave him a unique vantage point: a bird's-eye view of the whole globe, allowing him to make connections and see patterns that wouldn't have been clear to collectors on the ground. In this, Kew's Herbarium – the biggest in Britain, with both son and father in charge – was key. As Jim Endersby explains: 'The Herbarium gave Hooker the power to see the planet at a glance. Here, in the Herbarium, the chaos of nature was reduced to order.'

Hooker was interested in variation across the face of the earth. He was intrigued by patterns in the geographical distribution of species: for example, the way in which vegetation changed according to the climate across the globe, and the similarities and differences between the floras of different regions. He was also strongly influenced by the work of the great Prussian naturalist Alexander von Humboldt, who had spent five years in South America, between 1799 and 1804. Equipped with an impressive array of scientific instruments, Humboldt and his travelling companions set themselves the task of mapping the way in which temperature changed with altitude, for example, producing some of the first maps that showed distribution ranges.

Humboldt's geographical techniques immediately appealed to Hooker, who grasped that they could be used to produce clear, effective maps that showed species variation across different habitats. Hooker had a more profound aim: to make botany more scientific, converting it into a field of knowledge that could show genuine, precise causal laws, akin to Newton's in physics. At Kew, he set himself the task of creating and interpreting a collection with botanical authority to support his own theories. Darwin was open about his confidence in the younger man, writing: 'I know I shall live to see you the first authority in Europe on that grand subject, that almost keystone of the laws of creation, Geographical Distribution.' Today, Joseph Hooker is regarded as one of the founding fathers of biogeography, the discipline that seeks to understand the patterns and processes behind the geographical distributions of organisms.

Hooker's most important skill was his ability to classify plants. Like the modern-day taxonomists at work in the species identification meeting seen earlier, Hooker was adept at the fine detail of species identification, but also capable of seeing the big picture of patterns in plant diversity, creating overarching classifications of plant families and higher groups that remain in use today. As new specimens came in, he had very clear ideas about how to classify them. However, by his own account, his biggest problem was, unexpectedly, that of 'naturalists'.

In his view, naturalists read very little on botany, yet considered themselves experts. For Hooker, the greatest compliment a piece of scientific work could be paid was that it was 'philosophical', by which he meant that it was founded on sound, rigorous principles. He reported despondently, 'The study of botany is gradually taking a lower and lower place in our schools, and falls into the hands of a class of naturalists, whose ideas seldom rise above species, and who by what has well been called "hair splitting" tend to bring the study of these into disrepute.'

By 'hair splitting', Hooker was levelling an accusation that is still made in taxonomy today. Hooker himself was a 'lumper', who tended to define species as broadly as possible, by including in each one a great range of variation. The opposite of a lumper was a 'splitter', who would separate forms with slightly variant characteristics into a completely new, different species. As a self-diagnosed member of the 'lumping' camp, Hooker was exasperated by the botanists in obscure colonial outposts who sent 'new species' to Kew that he saw clearly occurring elsewhere. He once wrote wryly (and approvingly) of his colleague George Bentham, 'Well, he has turned out as great a lumper as I am.'

From all over the growing British Empire, thousands of naturalist missionaries, naturalist navy surgeons, and even, in Hooker's case, one naturalist bishop, were sending to Kew the plants they found. And in many cases, they were naming them as new species that, in Hooker's opinion, didn't display enough difference from others to be regarded as new. For him, time-wasting, in a discipline that was already so time-consuming, was the greatest possible crime. Worse still, it seemed to him that many of these correspondents were identifying new species simply for the glory of naming them.

His ambition, therefore, was to try to impose some sort of order from the centre, using the Kew collections to judge all these competing colonial claims. But Hooker's drive to establish Kew as a strong authority in the field was not without opposition. For example, William Colenso, Hooker's naturalist-missionary acquaintance on the other side of the world, felt strongly that he was much better equipped than Hooker to judge the specimens he found of New Zealand plants. Colenso had collected assiduously in his adopted homeland, eventually contributing some 6,000 New Zealand specimens to the Herbarium, but also sending Maori artefacts, such as a bottle gourd showing a Maori facial tattoo, to Kew's Museum of Economic Botany. Colenso, who was close to his Maori neighbours, became increasingly biased towards their native country. His botanical views were clear: New Zealand's flora was far richer than Hooker would ever allow. In the case of the New Zealand fern, *Lomaria procera*, for example, Colenso claimed there were sixteen different species, where Hooker saw only one.

Hooker eventually found Colenso's overconfidence tiring. 'From having no Herbarium,' he wrote to him crossly in 1854, 'you have described as new some of the best-known ferns in the world.' Yet Colenso did not give up; he was certain that fine detail in his specimens was lost when the plants were dried and stuck to herbarium sheets, then transported halfway around the world. He was passionate about local knowledge. One of his big enthusiasms was *Phormium tenax*, the New Zealand flax, an economic mainstay plant known as *harakeke* by the Maori, with many varieties that had hundreds of uses in native society. For Colenso, it was perfectly obvious that the variousness of these plants deserved the status of a 'species'. Hooker was not persuaded.

If he had accepted all the species proposed by colonial experts such as Colenso, the impact on the Herbarium would have been substantial, and the size of its collection would have outgrown any available building; this also provided a purely practical reason for Joseph Hooker's 'lumping' views. Jim Endersby explains: 'What Hooker was doing was comparing New Zealand's ferns to ferns from all over the southern hemisphere. And he could see there was a kind of gradual series, in which one form blends into another. So if you look at the series as a whole, spread out here on the floor of the Herbarium, there are no sharp breaks. And if there are no sharp breaks, then, in Hooker's mind, you cannot justify creating a species.'

So whilst Colenso argued that he knew best, looking at the living specimens in the field in New Zealand, Hooker remained sure that the only true way to define a species was by comparing specimens gathered from across the range of habitats it grew in, and the range of countries. In Jim Endersby's words: 'In some senses, Hooker was cut off from the plants he wanted to study . . . But by having them here in their dried and pressed form, as specimens, he was able to do things with them that he couldn't do out in the field.' For Hooker, only from Kew's central viewpoint could the competing claims be balanced and judged. He was occasionally almost joyful about the labour of the 'lumper'. 'It is wild and exciting work,' he wrote to George Bentham, 'the species go smash every day.'

Darwin hoped that Hooker would help him with examples for his 'big species book', which would eventually be published as *On the Origin of Species by Means of Natural Selection*. Darwin strongly suspected that natural selection would act upon species that possessed many different varieties and gradually develop them into multiple new species. However, Darwin also emphasised how slowly evolution progressed. Hooker concluded that many human lifetimes would pass before minor variations would evolve into genuinely separate species.

Today, Kew botanists still wrestle with the problems Hooker encountered, although these have been made far easier in recent years by DNA analysis. Mark Chase explains the botanical world's current view: 'What we are trying to do is to give a name – a sort of fixed concept – to something that is in fact an ongoing process: speciation. Plant species are not static – they are continually evolving, some going through periods of high diversification while others may be inching towards extinction. At this snapshot in time, though, we have to be able to describe plant diversity as we see it now. Different people will have different points at which they'll draw a line and say, "This is a species."'

Oct 17th - /79

DOWN,
BECKENHAM, KENT.
RAILWAY STATION
ORPINGTON. S.E.R.

My dear Hooker

I thank you heartily for your most kind congratulations about Horace; which rejoices us deeply. I happened to know of the reference to the work on statistics given me, I think, by Oliver's hand-writing. But I write now for the _chance_ of your having any or all of the 5 kind of seeds, on _next page_: I want much to see how the seedlings, which are so peculiar break through the ground. —

Ever yours

Ch. Darwin (over

Letter from Charles Darwin to Joseph Hooker requesting seeds,
17 October 1879

Tendencies to 'lump' and 'split' still remain within the taxonomic profession today, and the two approaches continue to be in tension. Nevertheless, for Hooker, botany's claim to be taken seriously as a science had to be based on establishing an internationally agreed system of naming, allowing natural history to take its place alongside chemistry and geology, as a newly serious and respectable academic field. In the end, Tim Utteridge's team in the sort meeting finally concluded that their white, marshmallowy find was not new to science: 'We found so many things overlapping with it in the Herbarium that we've just written it up to be published as a new note.' There is still no simple, easy answer, then, to that eternal question: where to draw the line.

6

TAMING THE EXOTIC

Underside of giant Amazonian waterlily pad,
William Sharp, 1854

IN KEW'S PRINCESS of Wales glasshouse, beyond tall stands of heliconias, lies a deep pool, around which large, whiskered fish languorously glide. In the pool's centre, five circular leaves cling to the water's surface, their colour ranging from pale green to dark red. Since being planted three months ago in January, the leaves have grown to 1.5 feet across but do not yet present much of a display. It will not be long before this plant is drawing the crowds, however, for it is *Victoria amazonica*, queen of the water-lilies. In just over a month, come summertime, its leaves will have grown to 10 feet across and its fragrant flowers will be opening up.

'It has very large, white flowers to start with, which open in the evening and have a smell of pineapple,' explains Lara Jewitt, Kew's Science Collections Coordinator. 'They also heat up, which invites a beetle to come and pollinate the plant. The flower closes around the beetle, then once it is pollinated, on the second night, the flower opens again. By this time it is pink in colour, has lost its smell of pineapple and the male parts of the flower have emerged. The beetle picks up the pollen and goes off to pollinate the next flower.'

One of the first Europeans to set eyes on this behemoth of the plant world, on the first day of 1837, was German-born surveyor Robert Schomburgk. Sent by the Royal Geographical Society (RGS) to inspect the network of waterways that crossed the nation's newly acquired territory of British Guiana, Schomburgk was having difficulties making headway on the river Berbice when he spotted an unusual object in the distance. When he urged his crew to paddle closer, he encountered 'a vegetable wonder', a waterlily bigger and more beautiful than anything he had seen before: 'A gigantic leaf, from five to six feet in diameter, salver-shaped, with a broad rim of light green above, and vivid crimson below, rested upon the water.' Even better, it was in bloom. The luxuriant flowers, each of which had many hundreds of petals, were coloured from pure white, to rose, to pink. The air was scented with their heady fragrance. 'All calamities were forgotten,' he wrote. 'I felt as [if I were] a Botanist, and felt myself rewarded.'

With little room in his *corial* (kayak) for such a vast plant specimen, Schomburgk was able to sample only a bud and a smallish leaf, which he packed into a barrel filled with brine. He also made detailed drawings of its parts, including seeds, buds and petioles (stalks that support leaves), before continuing on his way. He would carry the barrel with him for another three months before being able to despatch it – together with some 8,000 other plant specimens, bird skins, alligator skulls, insects, fossils and rocks – on a packet boat to England. Schomburgk had hatched the idea that the plant should be presented to Britain's heiress apparent, Princess Victoria, with a request to name it after her. By the time his specimens and papers arrived at the Royal Geographical Society two months later, the tribute seemed even more appropriate; Victoria had become Queen and the Society's new patron. Naming the flower would be a fitting tribute to the English rose of whom the nation expected so much.

Schomburgk, knowing that his new plant needed to be named by a botanist, had requested the RGS pass on the materials relating to his discovery to the Botanical Society of London. The Royal Geographical Society, however, was reluctant to do so, fearing that the botanists might steal its thunder. They therefore sent the specimen and its description to John Lindley (shortly to be called upon to write his report on Kew Gardens). As Assistant Secretary of the Horticultural Society and Professor of Botany at University College London, he was well qualified for the job. More importantly, he was one of the RGS's charter members. He could identify and name the plant for the RGS, after which the Society would send details of the new find to the Botanical Society. Schomburgk's notes and sketches, and the now rotting lily bud, were soon in Lindley's hands.

Schomburgk had believed his discovery to be a waterlily of the genus *Nymphaea*. However, when Lindley compared the descriptions to those of other *Nymphaea*, he was convinced the plant was not from that genus. It was also not a *Euryale*, another kind of waterlily that grew in the East. For this, Lindley must have been thankful, as the name 'Euryale' was that of the second eldest of the Gorgon sisters of Greek mythology, who had sharp fangs and snakes for hair. The Queen would surely not have been amused to have such a plant named after her. Lindley's final prognosis was that the plant belonged to a new genus thus far unknown to science: 'It appears to me that the object of its discoverer will be best attained by suppressing the name of *Nymphaea victoria* by which he had proposed to distinguish the plant, and by embodying Her Majesty's name in the usual way in that of the genus. I have therefore proposed to name it *Victoria regia*.' It was a good choice, for the Queen gave her approval.

When John Edward Gray, President of the Botanical Society of

London, eventually received the papers detailing the find, he was unaware that the Society had requested Lindley to identify the plant and therefore took it upon himself to classify it, independently naming it *Victoria regina*. Meanwhile, news came that the German botanist Eduard Poeppig had described a very similar plant, in 1832, growing in South America. He had named it *Euryale amazonica*. Discussions over what the correct name should be continued for a while but Lindley's version was most widely used until it was superseded by *Victoria amazonica* in the twentieth century. What the leading botanists of the day cared about more was getting their hands on some seeds so they could raise a living specimen. Writing for the *Gardener's Magazine and Register of Rural and Domestic Improvement* in 1837, the Scottish botanist and garden designer, John Claudius Loudon, gave voice to the general enthusiasm. 'We hope that this splendid plant will soon be introduced and that an aquarium worthy of Her Majesty, and of the advanced state of horticultural science, will be formed in the Botanic Garden at Kew for its reception.'

Building glasshouses to nurture growing plants was an emerging field of engineering in the early nineteenth century. Orangeries constructed in the eighteenth century to showcase exotics generally had a solid north wall and south-facing, wooden-framed windows. However, the arrival of the industrial revolution brought with it new possibilities. Wrought iron, which could now be produced more cheaply than in the past, provided a stronger, more malleable material than wood for manufacturing glazing bars, enabling a metal framework to be glazed on all sides. Loudon, an early innovator in glasshouse design, developed a zigzag 'ridge-and-furrow' roof design that maximised incoming light and, in 1816, patented a flexible wrought-iron glazing bar, which retained its strength when bent. Curved roofs and glass domes began springing up, as

The Great Conservatory at Chatsworth, Derbyshire,
designed by Joseph Paxton

these new materials and innovations were put to use. Within four years, the notable London nursery Messrs Conrad Loddiges and Sons, which specialised in exotics, could boast the largest curvilinear glasshouse in the country, a hothouse that was 80 feet long, 60 feet wide and 40 feet high.

In 1823, just as the glasshouse was emerging as the must-have garden accessory for the wealthy estate owner, ambitious young Joseph Paxton landed the job of head gardener for the Duke of Devonshire at Chatsworth, a stately home in Derbyshire. After repairing ornaments and improving the layout of the long-neglected gardens, Paxton began experimenting with growing fruits and vegetables under glass, improving the existing glass structures at Chatsworth and building new ones. He then set about reinventing Loudon's ridge-and-furrow construction. His refinements ensured that sunlight hit the glass perpendicularly in the mornings and evenings, maximising the light passing through it. The fierceness of the midday sun, meanwhile, was mitigated by the more oblique angle at which its rays hit the glass. This represented a revolution in glasshouse design.

In 1835, Paxton set about employing the knowledge and skills he had developed in working with glass in an ambitious project for a 'great stove', capable of enclosing huge tender plants from around the world. At 227 feet long, 123 feet wide and 67 feet high, it would cover an acre of ground and be topped with a curvilinear roof, showcasing his signature ridge-and-furrow design. The frame was to be built of wood, supported by iron columns. Subterranean boilers, fed with coal transported along hidden tunnels, would heat the glasshouse to tropical temperatures.

Early in 1836, while Robert Schomburgk was undertaking his explorations of British Guiana, the work began. Digging the foundations alone, just with shovels and wheelbarrows, took several months and it was three years before the building was ready to be glazed, with the largest panes of glass ever made. As Paxton's biographer, Kate Colquhoun, explains: 'It was a feat because it had to look beautiful; it was a feat because it was enormous; it was a feat because it provided horticultural theatre in effect, a place to house exotics from all around the world. When Darwin went to see it he said it was more like tropical nature than he had ever thought humanly possible.'

In 1840, the year Paxton's Great Stove was completed, Schomburgk sent a parcel of *Victoria regia* seeds to Chatsworth. Paxton tried to germinate them but failed. Then in 1846, William Hooker finally succeeded at Kew Gardens. The race to grow the Amazonian lily in England was won. Three years later, he had thirty or so seedlings to give away and Paxton was among the recipients.

Determined to win the competition to get *V. regia* to flower, Paxton built a tank in the Great Stove that would emulate the conditions of the plant's native tropical habitat. Heating pipes warmed the soil, small wheels kept the water moving and liquid sewage fed the seedling. When the plant was placed in the tank in early August, it had four leaves, around 6 inches across. By the beginning of October, one of the lily leaves had grown to 4 feet across, demanding a new, bigger tank. And at the beginning of November, the first bud appeared. A triumphant Paxton wrote to his employer, 'My Lord Duke, Victoria has Shewn flower! An enormous bud like a great poppyhead made its appearance yesterday morning and by this evening it looks like a large peach placed in a cup . . . no account can give a fair idea of the grandeur of its appearance.'

Paxton's success in coaxing the tropical plant to flower in November in England was ultimately made possible by the industrial revolution.

Glasshouses were increasingly popular: advertisement from
The Gardeners' Chronicle, 1876

It had provided a readily available supply of iron for the columns of the glasshouse, the innovation to make curved glass and the technology that powered the steam boilers. Pollution produced by industrialisation, meanwhile, helped to drive the uptake of glasshouses, as plants grown under glass were protected from soot. Paxton realised that the plant that his Great Stove had nurtured could, in turn, help improve glasshouse technology even further. When the *London Illustrated News* sent a reporter to cover Paxton's blooming success, he demonstrated the strength of the great plant's leaves by placing his young daughter, Annie, on a tin tray laid on one of them. It took her weight without any difficulty, giving Paxton an idea. Maybe he could emulate the design of the waterlily leaf to inject even greater strength into his glasshouse designs.

The lily's natural engineering was just the sort of thing to excite and inspire the enquiring Victorians. Even in its native tributaries of the Amazon, explorers admired and noted what they saw as its extraordinary architecture. British botanist Richard Spruce, who travelled in the Amazon and Andes between 1849 and 1864, even drew parallels between the plant and products of human industry. 'A leaf, turned up, suggests some strange fabric of cast-iron, just taken from the furnace, its ruddy colour, and the enormous ribs with which it is strengthened, increasing the similarity.'

Back in England, Paxton was drawing on the natural design of the bracing ribs on the underside of the lily leaf to design a new glasshouse specifically to house *Victoria regia*. The leaf had cantilevers radiating from its centre, with large bottom flanges and very thick middle ribs with cross-girders, which stopped the leaf from buckling as it floated on the water's surface. Paxton's Lily House imitated this natural feat of engineering, its flat ridge-and-furrow roof acting like the leaf's strong cross-girders. When a new building was mooted, to hold the Great Exhibition of the Works of Industry

Joseph Paxton's Crystal Palace, designed and constructed for the
Great Exhibition of 1851

of All Nations, to be held in 1851, Paxton mulled over the possibility of using the Lily House design, multiplied many times over, to create a vast structure. In the end, his plans for the building, which would be 1,848 feet long, 456 feet wide at its widest extent and 108 feet high, were approved. Informed by years of experience and the unique structure of the *V. regia* leaf, Paxton created, in London, the greatest glass building the world had ever seen, the Crystal Palace.

When the Great Exhibition opened, it showcased objects from the Empire and beyond, including a life-size, wax replica of the *Victoria regia* plant. Not only could wealthy horticulturalists now experience this wonder from the Amazon, so too could the general public. The *London Illustrated News* commented on the replica's similarity to the real plant, reporting: 'I chanced to have seen the flower itself in bloom at the botanic gardens only the day before and an imitation more faithful it would be difficult to imagine. There is – flower bud leaf – with the blue and white water lilies surrounding it like maids of honour in waiting upon a queen.'

By coaxing the Queen's waterlily to germinate and flower, far from the steamy heat of its Amazonian motherland, Kew Gardens' William Hooker and Chatsworth's Joseph Paxton had helped tame the rainforest in the public imagination and prompted a fascination for the plant that still draws crowds to Kew today. Now, the Crystal Palace, incorporating the natural strength of the giant plant, brought the entire British Empire and all its possibilities for commerce to the people under a single glittering roof.

7

TAPPING INTO
RUBBER

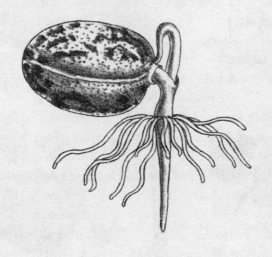

Hevea brasiliensis Müll. Arg.

Hevea brasiliensis, rubber plant, 1887

R UBBER WAS ONE of the British Empire's greatest commercial successes. Where would we be without it? Certainly not driving cars to work, wearing protective surgical gloves, playing tennis or communicating via a global telecommunications network. This ubiquitous substance is used for everything from energy generation and construction to aerospace and fashion. Turn back the clock a mere 150 years, however, and today's global rubber industry had yet to emerge. At that time, trees yielding the milky fluid we now know as latex grew wild in South America. It was to take an audacious plan by the British government, involving the 'theft' of seeds by a Kew Gardens plant hunter from the Amazonian rainforest, to turn rubber into the major commodity we rely on today.

Some 3,000 years ago, Mesoamericans used latex from various plant species to make balls, toys and the squeezy bulbs of syringes. The Spanish became aware of the substance after they started colonising the Americas in 1492. In 1615, the chronicler Juan de Torquemada reported that Spaniards in Mexico had learned to waterproof capes using the white juice of a tree. And in 1653, the priest Bernabé Cobo described coating stockings in latex to protect his legs when in the tropical jungle. However, Europeans showed little interest in the substance until 1736, when the naturalist Charles Marie de la Condamine first described the plant *Hévé* (which we now know was *Castilla elastica*, the Panama rubber tree) and the sticky *cahuchu* or *caoutchouc* it yielded.

A few years later, another Frenchman, François Fresneau, described latex and wrote of its potential uses in the West. The Scotsman Charles Macintosh was among the first Europeans to exploit its potential. By this time, latex was being used in Britain to erase pencil marks, an application that gave rise to the name 'India rubber', as early explorers referred to the natives of South America as 'Indians'. However, Macintosh became interested in the moisture-repelling qualities that had impressed the early travellers to South America. He discovered he could dissolve the solid India rubber derived from the liquid latex in coal naphtha and make fabric waterproof by dipping it in the solution. He patented 'Macintosh's waterproof double texture', which comprised two pieces of rubber cloth stuck together by an inner layer of rubber. In 1823, the waterproof mackintosh coat was born. This was a major advance, given that most coats at the time were made of absorbent wool or cotton.

Rubber presented one problem, though, which was its sensitivity to extremes of temperature. Mailbags made for the US post office in Boston by another rubber pioneer, Charles Goodyear, were rendered unusable when either the summer heat made them too sticky or the winter cold made them too brittle. Only when Goodyear heated sulphur and lead with rubber, in 1839, did he create a durable, stable material. Thomas Hancock, who had joined forces with Macintosh to work on perfecting rubber for coats, developed a similar process in the UK. Named 'vulcanisation' after Vulcan, the Roman god of fire, the new process promoted rubber to the status of a lucrative commodity. Its possibilities seemed

Linnaea borealis (twinflower), signature plant of great Swedish
taxonomist Carl Linnaeus who promoted its use to make
Lapp tea, described by his son as 'rather repulsive'

Famous cycad (*Encephalartos altensteinii*) resident at Kew since 1775.
One of the oldest pot plants in the world, it was brought back from
its native South Africa by collector Francis Masson

Stapelia gordonii from *Stapelia Novae; or a collection of several new species of that genus, discovered in the interior parts of Africa* (1796) by Francis Masson, Kew's first plant collector, sent by Sir Joseph Banks (Kew's de facto first Director) to the Cape of Good Hope with Captain James Cook

Stewartia malacodendron (silky stewartia or silky camellia tree) named
by Carl Linnaeus, painted by Georg Dionysius Ehret (1708–70),
renowned artist, collaborator and friend of Linnaeus

The herbarium of
Sir Joseph Banks
at his house in
central London.
Sepia painting by
Francis Boott, 1820

Mahogany shelves and
drawers of Carl Linnaeus's
library and collections at the
Linnean Society of London

Tiger lily (*Lilium tigrinum*) and double yellow Banksian rose (*Rosa banksiae*), first collected by the young plant hunter William Kerr in China, on expedition under the instruction of Sir Joseph Banks

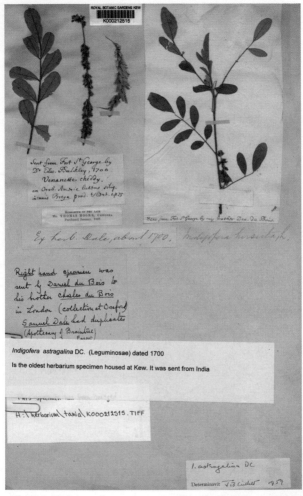

The Kew Herbarium houses over 7.5 million dried plant specimens, known as herbarium vouchers or sheets. This is the oldest at Kew, dated 1700, originally from the Dale Herbarium, and shows *Indigofera astragalina*, a member of the bean and pea family from India. Like many sheets it has been annotated over time

Dracaena kaweesakii (Kaweesak's dragon tree), a new species from Thailand, given its first scientific name in 2013. The specimen label details where it was collected, its plant description, local vernacular name, the ecology of its surroundings as well as the date and the collectors' names

DNA analysis has revealed surprising new relationships between plants: the poinsettia (*left*), with one of the world's smallest flowers (grouped within little yellow structures at the centre of the plant), and the tropical Asian *Rafflesia*, the corpse flower (*below*), which has one of the largest individual flowers reaching one metre across and smelling of rotting flesh

endless; it could be used to fashion everything from elasticised fabrics to insulation for undersea cables.

In 1851, the general public were invited to see the emerging range of items being produced across the British Empire and beyond, at the Great Exhibition of the Works of Industry of All Nations, held in Joseph Paxton's Crystal Palace in Hyde Park, London. (The palace was later moved to Sydenham, where its ruins remain.) Among the exhibits were rubber items produced by Macintosh, Hancock and Goodyear. Goodyear's stand comprised a series of rooms made entirely of vulcanite, a hard form of rubber. The display also showcased decorative items, including jewellery, tobacco pipes and a fruit bowl. These exhibits demonstrated to the Great Exhibition's 6 million visitors just how versatile rubber could be.

Prince Albert was a key driving force behind the exhibition and a keen promoter of the arts and sciences; London's Natural History Museum and Royal Albert Hall were among the institutions founded with the Prince's support, using profits from the Great Exhibition. When he and Queen Victoria stopped to look at Macintosh's stand, they were presented with a tablet of vulcanised rubber engraved with lines from William Cowper's poem *Charity*:

> *Again—the band of commerce was design'd*
> *T' associate all the branches of mankind,*
> *And if a boundless plenty be the robe,*
> *Trade is the golden girdle of the globe:*
> *Wise to promote whatever end he means,*
> *God opens fruitful Nature's various scenes,*
> *Each climate needs what other climes produce,*
> *And offers something to the gen'ral use . . .*

At this time many of the most valuable commodities on earth came from plants; tea, coffee, sugar, tobacco, cotton and jute were among them. Presenting the poem to the royals was a brilliant public relations exercise; its words captured the moment, giving credence to the notion that trading in God's abundant, worldwide, natural resources for the common good was a noble endeavour. With slavery only recently abolished, in 1833, some individuals even considered such trade a duty. While wealth made from sugar had been built on slavery, it was believed that 'legitimate commerce' in other plant products could help nurture fellowship between people from different parts of the globe.

By the middle of the nineteenth century, Kew Gardens was regularly receiving shipments of new and unusual plants sent by an international community of botanists. As well as examining and identifying these specimens, Kew's experts would assess their economic potential. The government wanted Kew to raise seedlings of commercially viable species and send them to the botanical gardens that it had set up in the colonies to develop these potential crops into whole plantations. Clements Markham, of the India Office, had already transferred cinchona, used to treat malaria (explained in more detail in Chapter 15), from South America to India and Ceylon, secretly defying the wishes of various South American governments. With the new-found demand for rubber products boosted by the success of the Great Exhibition, sourcing seeds from latex-yielding plants became a high priority for the government.

This urgency was exacerbated by reports from South America that the numbers of rubber trees there were dwindling, chiefly because the people who obtained latex from the rubber trees, known as 'tappers', often stripped off all the bark in the process. Although this had the desired effect of causing the latex to leak out, ready for collection, it also frequently killed the tree. As demand increased, so tappers had to travel farther to find new trees, pushing up prices. Plant collector Richard Spruce wrote in his journal that, by 1853, the price of rubber in Pará (in northern Brazil) rose so high that 'the mass of the population put itself in motion to search out and fabricate rubber'. He noted that 25,000 people were employed by the rubber industry in that small province alone. So many Pará workers downed their usual tools in favour of working with rubber that sugar, rum and *farinha* (flour) had to be imported from elsewhere.

Correspondence in Kew's archives shows that its Director, Joseph Hooker, favoured *Hevea brasiliensis* over other latex-yielding species. In late 1874 the British government sanctioned Henry Wickham, a wanderer whose career had included growing coffee in Brazil and trading bird skins in Central America, to collect '10,000 or more seeds', at a rate of £10 per 1,000 seeds. Wickham's somewhat weak credentials were that he had previously offered his

Drawing by Henry Wickham of 'My rancho, during the
India rubber season, Upper Orinoco', 1872

plant-collecting services to Kew and had demonstrated some knowledge of rubber in his book *Rough Notes of a Journey through the Wilderness, from Trinidad to Para*. In January 1876, the negotiations over Wickham's fee having been somewhat protracted, he finally wrote to confirm, 'I am just about to start for the "Curinga" districts in order to get you as large a supply of the fresh India rubber seeds as possible.'

The British government had originally intended that its rubber resources be developed in India. In 1873, Kew had received 2,000 *Hevea* seeds from Brazil on the instructions of James Collins, Curator of the Pharmaceutical Society and the author of several papers covering the history, commerce, supply and tapping of rubber. Kew's gardeners had germinated a few of the seeds and sent the young plants to Calcutta (now Kolkata) and Burma (now Myanmar). However, Calcutta's climate proved too dry, prompting Collins to suggest that Kew obtain more seeds and try growing them in Ceylon (now Sri Lanka) and Malacca (now a state of Malaysia; then part of the Straits Settlements).

It is odd that Kew entrusted Wickham to gather the seeds for them, when Hooker knew so little of his botanical expertise. However, Hooker was under pressure from the India Office to obtain *Hevea* seeds and Wickham was in the right place at the right time. He fulfilled his brief, packing up 70,000 seeds into crates that he declared to customs officers as being 'exceedingly delicate botanical specimens specially designated for delivery to Her Britannic Majesty's own Royal Garden at Kew'. In Wickham's personal account of his endeavours, he made much of having 'smuggled' the seeds out of Brazil. This tale has endured down the years, backed up by the fact that the Brazilians branded him a thief for carrying out an exploit 'hardly defensible in international law'. However, unsporting though it may have been, no laws forbidding the export of plant material existed at that time. Neither had the Brazilians been against a spot of seed 'thievery' themselves, when taking spice seeds from Cayenne in French Guiana to Pará in 1797.

Rubber seeds deteriorate rapidly and of the 70,000 that Wickham supplied, only around 4 per cent germinated. His commission could have been considerably more successful had he been asked to supply seeds that were still alive and therefore capable of germinating, but for some reason this detail was omitted from his contract. Nonetheless, in 1876, a total of 1,919 plants, grown from Wickham's 70,000 *Hevea brasiliensis* seeds, along with thirty-two seedlings of *Castilla elastica*, were on board the SS *Duke of Devonshire* bound for Colombo, Ceylon. They were received at Peradeniya Botanical Garden, Kandy, by the Superintendent, George Thwaites, who confirmed their safe arrival to Hooker: 'You will be rejoiced [sic] to hear that the Hevea and Castilloa [sic] plants have arrived in very fair order indeed. Ninety per cent will then little doubt be saved out of the Hevea collection and we have 28 out of the 31 Castilloa [sic] looking green and promising.'

When the gardeners in Ceylon noted that rubber plants at Peradeniya suffered in the wind of the dry north-eastern monsoon, they moved the *Hevea* plants to the newly founded Henarathgoda Botanical Gardens, which lay closer to Colombo and at a lower altitude. According to Kew's records, fifteen years after planting, the trunk of one of the Henarathgoda trees had grown in circumference to '6ft. 5in. at a yard above the ground'. It had been tapped just three times, yielding 1 lb 11¾ oz in 1888, 2 lb 10 oz in 1890 and 2 lb 13 oz in 1892. Henry Trimen, who had succeeded Thwaites in 1880, wrote: 'The tree is in no respect the worse for this treatment; the rest in alternate years permitting the scars from the trunk to become completely healed.'

The year after Kew had shipped its first rubber plants to Ceylon,

Henry Ridley (*left*) displaying the herring-bone pattern used
when tapping a rubber tree

twenty-two were sent from there to the Singapore Botanic Gardens. Henry J. Murton, who was in charge of the Gardens, planted eight of them in these grounds and the rest on other parts of the Malay peninsula. Murton's successor planted up another 1,200 from seeds of the initial stock. What remained of this planting was inherited by Henry Ridley, who took over as Director of the Singapore Botanic Gardens in 1888. At Hooker's urging, Ridley directed his efforts towards a study of rubber trees. His first task was to tame the overgrown rubber plantation, which he described as being a dense scrub abounding with snakes, including 27-foot pythons.

Ridley's experiments revealed that trees produced a constant amount of rubber over a twenty-four-hour period, and also that the renewed bark covering the wounds made by the 'tappers' contained as much latex as the original. This meant trees could be tapped daily for many years. He used a 'herringbone' method of extraction, which involved cutting a vertical groove and then making two paper-thin lateral cuts. Latex flowed from the side openings into the vertical groove and down to a cup affixed at the base. The cup was emptied into a milk can treated with acetic acid, which separated out the rubber as a white cream. This was rolled out flat, smoked to prevent mildew, then dried ready for export.

By now rubber was becoming sought after for an increasing range of products. In June 1890, the *India-Rubber and Gutta-Percha and Electrical Trades Journal* reported that the manufacturers of rubber tennis shoes had been unable that spring to meet the demand for their goods, declaring: 'Rubber is strong and advancing. What little there is of it is held in a few hands, and the market is almost sure to go higher. There is scarcely any prospect at all of its declining even after most of the goods have been made for the present season.'

Kew's annual report of 1882 had proudly reported that the 'task

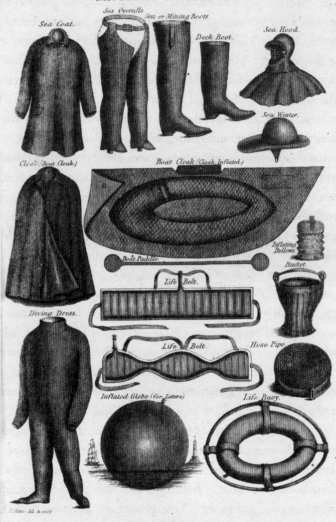

Sea Coat. · Sea Overalls · Sea or Mining Boots. · Deck Boot. · Sea Hood. · Sou Wester. · Cloak (Boat Cloak.) · Boat Cloak (Cloak Inflated.) · Inflating Bellows. · Boat Paddle. · Bucket. · Life Belt. · Diving Dress. · Life Belt · Hose Pipe · Inflated Globe (for Letters) · Life Buoy.

Selection of nautical articles made from India rubber, 1857

initiated by the India Office has now been successfully accomplished'. However, even greater commercial success was still to come. In 1893, rubber brokers Hecht, Levis & Kahn assessed a sample of Ceylon rubber that Kew had sent them, writing that the quality was 'very good indeed, and the curing of the same seems to have been effected in the proper manner'. Most importantly, they confirmed that it 'would be easily saleable in large quantities'. As demand for the new, versatile material rose, rubber superseded tea as Ceylon's main crop.

Across the Indian Ocean in Singapore, 'Rubber' or 'Mad' Ridley, as he had by now become known, forecast that the demand for rubber would soon outstrip supply. Such was his conviction that he filled the pockets of visiting district officers and planters with seeds to plant around their houses. At first, few were interested but that changed after planter Tim Bailey made £500,000 from rubber in a few years. As Ridley recalled, 'everyone went mad, estates came up everywhere, every bit of waste ground, orchards and even gardens were planted up, no one talked of anything else'. When two steamers carrying the Brazilian crop sank in the Amazon, the price of rubber rocketed. The Malaysian rubber industry, which had begun with just twenty-two plants grown on the back of experiments by Kew gardeners, virtually destroyed the Brazilian trade almost overnight.

Today, in the chilled store of Kew's Economic Botany Collection, rubber items from the Great Exhibition are preserved for posterity, clearly showing the versatility of the newly perfected material. One box contains jewellery from Goodyear's collection of ebonite, a hard, black form of rubber. There are chain-link bracelets, knot earrings and an oval brooch that depicts two deer, complete with intricately moulded antlers. Another box, containing four grey gaskets, highlights the less glamorous but more important use of rubber in the steam industry: to connect the iron or steel pipes used in steam engines. As Mark Nesbitt, Curator of the Collection, points out: 'There were all kinds of mundane but extremely important industrial uses of rubber.'

Designed to show what the new-found miracle material of rubber was capable of, these items recall the prosperity, hope and entrepreneurial spirit of the days of Empire. Whatever we may think of the Victorians' ethics in taking commercially valuable plants from other nations and cultivating them in their own colonies to trade the commodities derived from them, it was their vision and perseverance that gave rise to today's multi-billion-dollar rubber industry and the myriad products it provides. Synthetic rubber production overtook that from plantations in the 1950s, but natural rubber still accounts for around 40 per

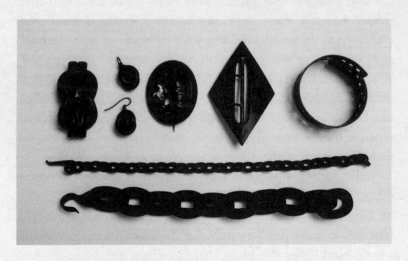

Items from Charles Goodyear's collection of ebonite for the
Great Exhibition, 1851, from Kew's Economic Botany Collection

cent of global production. Had the likes of Hooker, Wickham and Ridley not recognised the potential of the *Hevea* tree and its latex sap, our journeys through life would be wetter, bumpier, noisier and more dangerous by far.

8

ORCHIDMANIA

Nineteenth-century orchidmania: advertisement
for sale of imported orchids

THE DAYS OF tropical plants being unobtainable rarities are long gone. Anyone with a few pounds to spare can buy an orchid. Growers have perfected the process of germinating the thousands of tiny seeds produced by each seed pod from *Phalaenopsis*, *Cymbidium* and *Dendrobium* orchids, enabling them to grow the plants in their millions and sell them to the public for a handsome profit. As a result, we are now able to pop into our local garden centre or supermarket and pick up a piece of tropical paradise whenever we want. Many people do just that; *Phalaenopsis* has, more than once, received from the Flowers and Plants Association the accolade of Britain's most popular houseplant. Kew's annual Orchids Festival, meanwhile, enables people to experience more unusual orchids in a tropical environment. 'The orchid has this fantastic, exotic, sometimes sexual, connotation,' says Emma Townshend, a volunteer guide at Kew Gardens. 'Some people just want to go and look at the incredibly colourful *Vanda* plants, hanging down from the ceiling. Other people like the tiny details of the temperate orchids in the cool orchid room. And for some people, when they put their face up to a rare scented orchid and breathe in that perfume, you can see that their day has really been changed. People perceive the orchid to be the height of luxury.'

It hasn't always been so easy to enjoy these exotic blooms. The *Encyclopaedia Londinensis, Or, Universal Dictionary of Arts, Sciences and Literature* reported in 1810 that although numerous species of the tropical *Epidendrum* orchids had been introduced into British gardens from the tropical and subtropical Americas, it required great skill and attention to overcome the difficulties of cultivating such 'parasitical' plants. This term referred to the fact that most tropical orchids are epiphytes (in fact not parasites), growing on other plants while deriving their moisture and nutrients from the air, rainfall and vegetal debris around them.

Initially, growers were unsure how to provide suitable conditions for these so-called 'air plants' in their hothouses. Eventually, in 1787, Kew botanists coaxed the tropical orchid *Prosthechea cochleata*, or cockleshell orchid, to bloom for the first time in Britain. When news spread of this and other horticulturalists' early successes with orchids, every botanical enthusiast in Britain was desperate to try cultivating the mysterious plants, which thrived high up in the forest canopy, without visible nourishment, in some of the most remote and beautiful regions on earth.

By the early nineteenth century, *Curtis's Botanical Magazine, Or, Flower-garden Displayed* was able to report that many species of the *Epidendrum* genus 'had been brought to flower in great perfection'. Soon, Loddiges and Sons were helping to fuel interest in orchids by cultivating and selling them from their nursery in Hackney, London. With the abolition of the so-called 'window' tax in 1845, and the invention of a new manufacturing system that enabled large sheets of glass to be made very cheaply, more and more people could afford to have a glasshouse in their back garden and to fill it with exotic plants. The possession of such a luxury, until very recently confined to the richest and highest echelons of society, was a prized sign of social success. Everybody had to have an orchid. Plant hunters, scouring the world's wildest areas to gather exotic plants for botanical gardens and private collectors, focused more closely on these alluring blooms. 'Orchidmania' was born.

Tales of how some of the world's loveliest orchids had arrived on British shores were published in the weighty and lavishly illustrated tome *The Orchidaceae of Mexico and Guatemala*, by plantsman and garden designer James Bateman, between 1837 and 1843. Bateman described orchids as 'the chosen ornaments of royalty', neatly capturing the allure of the potent mixture of imperial conquest and scientific study. His fascination with these beautiful plants is reported to have begun at around eight years of age, passed on by his parents. Later, whilst studying at the University of Oxford, he visited Thomas Fairburn's nursery when he should have been attending lectures. Here he saw the orchid *Renanthera*

Cartoon by George Cruikshank of James Bateman's huge tome
The Orchidaceae of Mexico and Guatemala, 1837–43

coccinea for the first time, as well as observing a picture of it in bloom, later recalling: 'Of course, I fell in love at first sight, and as Mr Fairburn asked only a guinea for his plant (high prices were not yet in vogue), it soon changed hands and travelled with me to Knypersley, when the Christmas holidays began. I had caught my orchid, but how to treat it I knew not.'

The populace's appetite for orchids was fed by George Ure Skinner, a voracious collector from Manchester who owned extensive estates in Guatemala and was responsible for introducing almost 100 new orchid species into cultivation in Britain, among them the pink-petalled *Guarianthe skinneri*, which bears his name. The botany of this Central American country was relatively unknown to the British until Skinner was requested to send some specimens. Bateman reports on Skinner's valiant efforts in *The Orchidaceae of Mexico and Guatemala*:

> From the moment he received our letter, he has labored [sic] almost incessantly to drag from their hiding places the forest treasures of Guatemala, and transfer them to the stoves [hothouses] of his native land. In pursuit of this object, there is scarcely a sacrifice which he has not made, or a danger or hardship which he has not braved. In sickness or in health, amid the calls of business or the perils of war, whether detained in quarantine on the shores of the Atlantic, or shipwrecked on the rocks of the Pacific, he has never suffered an opportunity to escape him of adding to the long array of his botanical discoveries!

Skinner spent more than thirty years as a plant collector, during the course of which he crossed the Atlantic thirty-nine times. Fate struck at the very end of his last trip; on the day of his departure from Panama, he fell ill with yellow fever and died two days later.

It was the glamorous *Cattleya labiata* species that particularly ignited enthusiasm for orchid collecting in Britain. The naturalist William Swainson had been the first person to collect specimens, in 1818, during a collecting trip to Pernambuco in Brazil. William Cattley, a grower and introducer of tropical plants, nurtured a specimen of it that was sent to him and was rewarded with a large, trumpet-like bloom. It is now named after him.

A few other *Cattleya* specimens were coaxed to flower, causing a sensation among horticulturalists and fuelling a demand that was thwarted by the fact that no one knew exactly where Swainson had gathered the originals. At that time there were often no maps available to collectors of the terrain being explored, leaving them therefore with no means of pinpointing exactly where finds were made. When naturalist George Gardner travelled to Brazil some eighteen years later, he thought he had located specimens in two places: on Gavea, or Topsail, Mountain and across from it on the neighbouring peak, Pedra Bonita. However, these later turned out to be a different species, *Cattleya lobata*.

The ravishing *C. labiata* continued to prove elusive. It was not until many decades later, in 1889, that it was finally rediscovered in Pernambuco. Its re-emergence encouraged the collecting mania for these plants.

The first orchid-growing society was founded in Manchester in April 1897, with more soon opening up all over Britain. With orchid cultivation now within reach of a wider range of people and increasingly popular, nurseries could make a handsome profit by collecting large volumes of plants. They sent plant hunters out in droves; in 1894 one nursery alone despatched twenty collectors to the world's jungles. The result was that natural populations of sought-after species became greatly depleted. Kew Director Joseph Hooker was

CYPRIPEDIUM GODEFROYÆ.

Price 42s. each.

For full description, *see* page 19.

Veitch catalogue from 1886 offering orchids for sale,
this one at 42 shillings each

dismayed by the scale of orchid collecting. He ruefully described having seen collectors from the Royal Botanic Garden, Calcutta (now Kolkata), filling hundreds of baskets with them:

> What with Jenkins' and Simon's collectors here, twenty or thirty of Falconer's, Lobb's, my friends Kaban and Cave and Inglis' friends, the roads here are becoming stripped like the Penang jungles, and I assure you for miles it sometimes looks as if a gale had strewed the road with rotten branches and Orchideae. Falconer's men sent down 1000 baskets the other day, and assuming 150 at the outside as the number of species worth cultivating, it stands to reason that your stoves [hothouses] in England will still be stocked. The only chance of novelty is in the deadly jungles of Assam, Jyntea, and the Garrows. I am therefore not spending my money on Orchideae collecting but rather on Palms, Scitamineae, &c., which are more difficult to procure and not sought after by these plunderers.

Subsequent research has shown that, in order to thrive, orchids are dependent on specific pollinators that, in turn, contribute vital services within ecosystems. In other words, if you remove orchids from a habitat, as well as the plants that they rely on for survival, you prevent that ecosystem from functioning healthily. Charles Darwin was among the first men of science to make the connection between orchids and their habitats, noting that certain orchids had evolved blooms that would allow only a specific pollinator to access their pollen.

'Darwin realised two very important things,' explains Jim Endersby. 'One is that the traditional explanation for the exotic and extravagant beauty of flowers, which is that God made them to delight us, clearly doesn't hold. But what's much more interesting is that the theory of evolution by natural selection explains the bizarre diversity of orchid forms because that's how you account for this lock-and-key fit between the insect and its flower.'

Three years after writing *On the Origin of Species*, putting forward the idea that plants and animals evolved though natural selection rather than being created, Darwin became increasingly fascinated with orchids, which he described as being 'universally acknowledged to rank amongst the most singular and most modified forms in the vegetable kingdom'. Examining and experimenting on the many varieties native to Britain and then broadening his scope across the world – aided in his work by his family, friends and a wide circle of correspondents (including Joseph Hooker) – Darwin took full advantage of the contemporary vogue for growing exotic orchids. In 1862 he published *The Various Contrivances by which Orchids are Fertilised by Insects*, commonly known as *Fertilisation of Orchids*. This provided evidence for the process of natural selection. In this he explained that the array of forms taken by orchid blooms was a direct result of relationships between plants and their insect pollinators.

One way some orchids lure insects to them is by producing nectar. When an insect inserts its proboscis into a bloom to take out the nectar, it inadvertently takes pollen away with it. Then, when the insect goes on to visit another orchid of the same species, it pollinates it. It is an advantage for a plant to have a close relationship with a specific pollinator, because although this means it has fewer of them, the insects that do come will go on to visit only plants of the same species. As a result, less pollen will be wasted (most plants are infertile to pollen from other species). The adaptation also benefits the insect, since it is less likely to be competing with other insect species for that particular orchid's nectar.

In 1862, James Bateman sent Darwin specimens of the orchid

Cockroaches not orchids! George Cruikshank's cartoon in
Bateman's *The Orchidaceae of Mexico and Guatemala* showed the
hazards of importing exotic plants

Angraecum sesquipedale, which has stunning trumpet-like flowers that
open in a star shape. Darwin wrote to Joseph Hooker, saying, 'I have
just received such a Box full from Mr Bateman with the astounding
Angraecum sesquipedalia [sic] with a nectary [nectar-producing plant
tissue] a foot long. Good Heavens what insect can suck it.' In a
second letter a few days later, he was still thinking about it, suggesting
that 'in Madagascar there must be moths with probosces [sic] capable
of extension to a length of between ten and eleven inches [25.4–27.9
centimetres]'. Essentially, Darwin was predicting that the long, nectar-
producing spur of the orchid must be pollinated by a moth with a
tongue of equal length. In 1907, twenty-five years after his death,
a moth exhibiting such characteristics, named *Xanthopan morganii*
subspecies *praedicta,* was found. However, not until 1992 were images

captured that showed the moth feeding from the plants and transferring their pollen from one orchid to another.

When Darwin set out his theory of evolution, the basic principles he proposed were regarded by some as conflicting with the prevailing religious beliefs of the time. He wrote in 1861, 'It really seems to me incredibly monstrous to look at an orchid as created as we now see it. Every part reveals modification on modification.' His studies of the fragile orchid helped to persuade others of the reality of evolution. The close relationships exhibited by orchids and their pollinators provided compelling evidence for natural selection being the mechanism by which evolution progressed. Thanks to the theory of evolution, scientists working in the life sciences could make verifiable predictions, giving their work more rigour and credibility. Writing in *Scientific American* in 2000, Ernst Mayr, one of the twentieth century's leading evolutionary biologists, declared that no biologist had been responsible for more – and for more drastic – modifications of the average person's world view than Charles Darwin.

Today, botanists estimate there to be some 30,000 orchid species on earth. Thanks to Darwin's, and others', studies, they know that the highly specific relationships that orchids have with pollinators have played a major role in the success of the orchid family.

However, such adaptations to very particular local conditions can make species highly vulnerable to sudden changes in their environment. Ghillean Prance (Kew's Director from 1988 to 1999) helped highlight this vulnerability when he conducted research into orchids and their ecological relationships in the Amazon rainforest.

Prance realised, for example, that a successful wild harvest of the commercially valuable Brazil nut (*Bertholletia excelsa*) was dependent on the health of the surrounding Amazon rainforest – including the orchids within it. The tree requires female euglossine bees to pollinate its flowers. These bees will mate only with males that have successfully gathered a cocktail of scents from several orchid species, all of which thrive solely in undisturbed forest. Such delicately balanced interdependencies between different plants and animals illustrate how precarious a foothold many orchids maintain in what the Victorians would have called the 'economy of nature'.

Today, Kew's Conservation Biotechnology team is continuing work to unravel the complex relationships between orchids and their habitats including in Madagascar, home of Darwin's famous deep-flowered orchid, and its friend, the long-tongued moth. Madagascar is extremely rich in orchid species, many of them at risk. The team is gathering seeds from around fifty rare orchids from the central highlands of the island, for propagation and cultivation at Kew. Orchids can produce tens of thousands of seeds per seed pod, each of which comprises an embryo and a surrounding seed coat. Unlike the seeds of most plants, orchid seeds have no built-in food supply (endosperm), so the embryo must obtain its food outside in order to germinate.

In the wild, orchids rely on the presence of specific fungi for germination, which grow in very close association with their roots (the fungi that truffle expert Albert Bernhard Frank named as mycorrhizae – see Chapter 4), thereby providing the developing plant with nutrients and carbohydrates that the seed is lacking, and promoting healthy growth in the young plants. In the laboratory, these carbohydrates and nutrients can be supplied to orchid seeds in simple forms that they can use without the presence of mycorrhizae. However, plants grown with the correct fungi tend to germinate more successfully and to grow more rapidly and healthily. The Kew team is currently collecting the fungi that the Madagascan orchids grow with in the wild, so as to replicate the relationship in their laboratory.

Orchid cultivation in the laboratory at Kew, a step towards
conserving rare orchids in the wild

In a laboratory inside Aiton House at Kew Gardens, hundreds
of transparent culture vessels (essentially, plant-containing pots)
are lined up on metal shelves in a climate-controlled room.
Viswambharan Sarasan, Head of Kew's Conservation Biotechnology
team, picks up two petri dishes containing *Cynorkis* orchid seedlings
to demonstrate the role played by fungi.

'Conventional orchid seed germination under laboratory conditions is conducted using a medium containing essential minerals,
vitamins, sugar and an organic supplement such as peptone, in
this case, for the seedlings to grow,' he explains, pointing to the
three or four tiny green shoots inside the dish. 'This means the
plants can develop even before they start photosynthesising [using
light energy to generate sugars that fuel the plant's growth, as
explained in Chapter 11] inside the culture vessels. However, under

the same environmental conditions, with no added minerals, sugar or other organic supplements but with the addition of a specific mycorrhizal fungus, the seeds germinate faster and there is a ten-fold increase in the number that grow,' he says, picking up the second pot. 'Look at the number of seedlings here. There must be nearly a hundred. The symbiotic fungus provides ideal conditions for the seeds to germinate and grow. Adding it produces more plants, faster, and their quality is far better.'

Learning how to grow orchids in the laboratory is a step towards conserving Madagascar's rare orchids in the wild. Eventually, the plan is that Kew's botanists will be able to raise these plants en masse in the laboratory and then grow them in the horticultural nursery, to help reintroduce species to the wild in a way that will allow them to become self-sustaining. With so many areas facing threats from logging, illegal plant collecting, mining and slash-and-burn agriculture, this is an essential step towards orchids once again thriving in their natural habitats.

'We are producing these symbiotic seedlings for large-scale reintroduction or restoration work,' says Sarasan. 'Madagascar is a very difficult place to work, in terms of regular monitoring, because of the vast terrains and costs involved. Therefore we need to make sure we put resilient plants back into their original habitat and that a natural rehabilitation process sets in. When we go back after six months or so, these seedlings should be there, growing away happily. The ultimate aim is to help establish laboratory-grown, symbiotic seedlings of rare and threatened orchids that will eventually produce self-sustaining populations in the wild. Only then will our work be complete.'

So, orchids are a paradox. The orchid plant family's intricate evolution has made it so successful that it is now the most diverse in the world. The family displays an incredible variety of shapes and forms, with blooms ranging from the showy *Cattleya* to the spider-shaped *Brassia* (the latter's shape assists its pollination by spider-hunter wasps – the wasp stings the lip while trying to grasp its supposed prey. The pollen is thus stuck to its head and when it flies to another *Brassia* flower, this flower gets pollinated). Orchids have beguiled millions of people down the centuries and continue to rate highly amongst gardeners today. Yet, simultaneously, they are among the most threatened plants on earth. And, encouraged by the early shifts of orchids around the globe, some orchids are now revealing a rather dark side to their character: that of botanical bully. For example, *Spathoglottis plicata*, an orchid native to Australia and in need of conservation there, is seen as an invasive plant in Puerto Rico, and is implicated in hindering the reproduction of that country's native orchid *Bletia patula*. As botanists have come to learn, one country's 'ornament of royalty' can be another nation's weed.

9
PLANT INVADERS

PL. VI.

J.D.H. delt.   John Murray, Albemarle Street, 1854.   W.L. Walton, lith.

Kinchinjunga from Singtam (Elevn 5000ft.) looking West.

Joseph Hooker encountered many previously unknown species
of rhododendron in the Himalaya

L ONG BEFORE CONRAD Loddiges founded his famous nursery in London, he was working as a gardener near Haarlem in the Netherlands. Among the exotics he grew was an attractive, mauve-flowering, evergreen shrub native to Turkey, the Caucasus and Spain. When Loddiges moved to England in 1761, he took with him some of its seeds and sowed them in the Hackney garden of lawyer Sir John Sylvester, his new employer. They were the first, but by no means the last, of its seeds to be grown in England. By the middle of the nineteenth century, Kew's Director William Hooker was able to report that 'it may probably be said with truth, that no kind of flowering shrub is so easily, and has been so extensively, cultivated, or has formed so vast an article of traffic, as that one oriental species to which the name seems more immediately to have been given, the *Rhododendron Ponticum* [sic].'

William was writing in the preface to his son Joseph Hooker's book *The Rhododendrons of Sikkim-Himalaya*. This lavish three-part volume, published between 1849 and 1851, showcased forty-three species of *Rhododendron* encountered by Joseph on his travels in Asia. In Joseph's letters he describes seeing these magnificent plants in the wild: 'The splendour of the Rhododendrons is marvellous: there are 10 kinds on this hill, scarlet, white, lilac, yellow, pink, marroon [sic]: the cliffs actually bloom with them.'

Joseph Hooker was thirty years old when he made his plant-collecting journey to India. He was keen to travel around and bring back plants from the tropics, following his earlier expedition to Antarctica. The destination choice was influenced by his father, William, who was always on the lookout for new plant introductions to the Gardens. Arriving in Darjeeling in 1848, Joseph was much impressed by the scenery and vegetation:

> I arrived at Darjeeling on a rainy misty day, which did not allow me to see ten yards in any direction, much less to descry the Snowy Range, distant sixty miles in a straight line. Early next morning I caught my first view, and I literally held my breath in awe and admiration. Six or seven successive ranges of forest-clad mountains, as high as that whereon I stood, intervened between me and a dazzling white pile of snow-clad mountains . . . The heavenward outline was projected against a pale blue sky; while little detached, patches of mist clung here and there to the highest peaks, and were tinged golden yellow, or rosy red, by the rising sun, which touched these elevated points long ere it reached the lower position which I occupied.

With the assistance of both local British residents and Lepcha porters (Lepchas, known as Rongpa in Sikkimese, were one of Sikkim's ethnic groups), Hooker was able to collect so many *Rhododendron* that his spoils ended up greatly increasing the number then in cultivation. Collecting them had been no easy task, though:

> I staid [sic] at 13000ft very much on purpose to collect there seeds of the Rhododendrons & with cold fingers it is not very easy . . . Botanizing, during the march is difficult. Sometimes the jungle is

so dense that you have enough to do to keep hat & spectacles in company, or it is precipitous . . . certainly one often progresses spread-eagle fashion against the cliff, for some distance, & crosses narrow planks over profound Abysses, with no hand-hold whatever.

There were political obstacles too. The Rajah of Sikkim, to the north of Darjeeling, was justifiably nervous of any British presence, fearful that it would provoke intervention from China. Pressed by the Indian government, he reluctantly allowed Hooker's party passage in 1849, on condition that they did not travel to the Tibetan passes. The lure of plants was too much for Hooker, however, who couldn't resist crossing the border into Tibet, finding more rhododendrons, as well as blue, pink and violet primulas. Laid under house arrest by the Rajah, Hooker and his travelling companion were released on the threat of a British invasion.

The detailed descriptions and beautiful illustrations in Hooker's book, hand-coloured by botanical artist Walter Hood Fitch, entranced horticulturalists and fuelled a craze for rhododendrons. Seeds from the Sikkim trip were passed on to twenty-one individuals, including Charles Darwin and Joseph Paxton; to eight European botanical gardens; to nineteen rhododendron gardens in Scotland, England and Ireland; and to eleven UK nurseries. The landed gentry, for whom the lush shrubs appeared to possess a grandeur befitting the magnificence of their estates, enthusiastically embraced growing and hybridising them. They used *R. ponticum* as a rootstock onto which to graft Hooker's Sikkim species; they also underplanted woodlands with it and, as shooting grew in popularity in the late 1860s, used it as heathland game cover.

Hooker, having seen the devastation caused by orchid hunters on his travels, was among the first botanists to ponder the long-term effects that humans might have on the world's flora. When

Rhododendron Dell at Kew in the Victorian era

a gallery opened at Kew in 1882, exhibiting the paintings of Marianne North, one of the best-travelled and most adventurous of botanical artists, he observed, with feeling:

> Visitors may, however, be glad to be reminded, that very many of the views here brought together represent vividly and truthfully scenes of astonishing interest and singularity, and objects that are amongst the wonders of the vegetable kingdom; and that these, though now accessible to travellers and familiar to readers of travels, are already disappearing or are doomed shortly to disappear before the axe and the forest fires, the plough and the flock of the ever advancing settler or colonist. Such scenes can never be renewed by nature, nor when once effaced can they be pictured to the mind's eye, except by means of such records as this lady has presented to us, and to posterity.

It is ironic, then, that in showcasing rhododendrons, Joseph Hooker inadvertently set in motion a chain of events that would still be wreaking havoc in the British countryside some 165 years later. For, as his father William had noted, *Rhododendron ponticum* needed little help to get established in the UK. It not only produces millions of seeds, but also spreads by putting out suckers from its roots, and by layering (forming roots) where its branches touch the ground. As it happily settled into its new location and multiplied generously, it eventually switched status from being an attractive exotic to an aggressive invader. As Jim Endersby points out: 'Large parts of England are now overrun with rhododendrons that, having escaped from people's gardens, have grown into impenetrable thickets, in some places even choking out native vegetation.'

Among the wave of exotics that were shifted about from nation to nation in the nineteenth century, rhododendrons were not alone in thriving in their new homes.

Many of today's worst 'weeds' started out as deliberate introductions. The very things that made them such spectacular trophy plants in gardens – their huge size, exotic flowers and vast leaves – also appear to have made them the perfect invaders. One of the culprits in the spread of a range of such plants was the 'Wild Garden' movement, instigated by the gardener and journalist William Robinson. Robinson disliked the repetitive nature of formal gardens, such as those planted around the Crystal Palace; instead he favoured establishing in his garden 'plant natures' from a variety of locations outside the British Isles. In his influential book *The English Flower Garden*, published in 1883, he laid out his idea of a wild garden, explaining: 'It is applied essentially to placing of perfectly hardy exotic plants in places and under conditions where they will become established and take care of themselves.' Vigorous, eye-catching plants like rhododendrons fitted the bill nicely.

'Garden terrace with free vegetation and informal arrangements',
from William Robinson's *The English Flower Garden*, 1883

The Wild Garden movement, plant hunters, nurseries and botanical gardens all played a major role in introducing some fairly troublesome invasive species. Their combined actions more than a century ago have left every country in the world with, on average, fifty seriously invasive species of plants and animals. Given the right conditions, alien plants can destroy an entire ecosystem by upsetting the fragile natural balance that exists between its plant, animal and fungal inhabitants. As Colin Clubbe, Head of Kew's UK Overseas Territories and Conservation Training, explains: 'When some of the most aggressive invasives are introduced to a very small area, their numbers can explode and have an impact extremely quickly, spreading rapidly and then outcompeting natives for nutrients or light, crowding them out, which can lead to the decline of species and even their extinction.'

Lantana camara is one botanical aggressor that does just that. This evergreen shrub, which has striking golden flowers and is grown as an ornamental shrub in Britain, possesses the key characteristics of the successful invader. It spreads rapidly, as it grows well on disturbed soil and if damaged will regenerate easily from the base. A native of South America, it was brought to Europe by Dutch explorers and was subsequently cultivated globally.

It was introduced to the botanical garden in Calcutta (now Kolkata) around 1807 as a hedge plant. A century later, Dietrich Brandis, a German working with the British Imperial Forestry Service in India, noted that the plant had spread with 'extraordinary vigour' in Ceylon (now Sri Lanka) and the Indian peninsula, becoming a 'most troublesome weed' in deciduous forests. Within another fifty years, the situation had worsened to the point that, according to forestry worker T. Jayadev, it had 'taken possession of the ground in dense impenetrable thickets in young teak plantations'. Despite attempts to uproot the plant, nothing seemed to eradicate it, and it remains problematic today. Estimates from India suggest the present cost of controlling *Lantana camara* is approximately 9,000 Indian rupees (£88) per hectare. There are now 650 hybrid varieties of *Lantana* causing mayhem across sixty countries and island groups.

Islands are particularly vulnerable to invasive species. After Joseph Hooker visited Ascension Island in 1876, he described its endemic (unique to the island) parsley fern (*Anogramma ascensionis*), a diminutive plant with delicate yellow-green leaves that resemble miniature sprigs of parsley. It was recorded again in 1889, but thereafter was largely forgotten about until British scientist Eric Duffey noted its occurrence in 1958 on the north side of Green Mountain. The plant was not then seen for several decades, despite repeated searches, and so scientists reluctantly declared it extinct in 2003. One reason put forward for its demise was the introduction of maidenhair ferns (*Adiantum* species), which have aggressively colonised the parsley fern's rock-ledge habitat. In 2010, however, when climbing a knife-edge ridge running down the southern slopes of Green Mountain, members of Ascension Island's Conservation Department spied a tiny fern leaf on a bare rock. Recognising it as the long-lost parsley fern, they looked for further specimens and discovered four minute plants.

The find prompted a conservation project in which spores from this frail colony were collected, placed in a sterile container, rushed to the island's airfield and then flown to RAF Brize Norton in Oxfordshire. A waiting car then transported the spores to Kew Gardens. Kew was able to rear a large number of plants, and the Ascension Island team also germinated some spores, growing them through into adult plants. The hope is that the partners can work together to, eventually, reintroduce the parsley fern to Ascension Island. First, though, they must tackle the problem of the invasive maidenhair fern.

'One of the things we're doing now, experimentally, is some small-scale clearance of the maidenhair fern in an effort to develop a suitable habitat for the parsley fern as a self-sustaining population in the wild,' explains Colin Clubbe. 'I think we're going to have to make these conservation interventions all the time, using horticultural skills in the field to try to maintain a balance of competing species, and actively intervening if we see the invasives are beginning to overwhelm the habitat.'

With attempts to eradicate invasive species often failing, and control programmes being exceedingly expensive to maintain, new approaches are required. In India, where (according to World

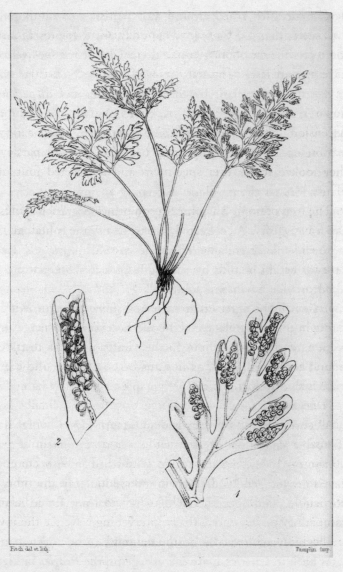

Fitch del et lith.   Pamplin imp.

The Ascension Island parsley fern, illustrated by W.H. Fitch

Bank figures for 2010) around 32.7 per cent of the population live on less than US $1.25 (73p) per day, the ever-present *Lantana* could provide the poorest people there with alternative livelihoods. Its berries are tasty to humans (as well as to the birds that continue to distribute the plant by eating its berries and dispersing the enclosed seeds far and wide), so could be used to make marmalade or jam. Meanwhile, there is also potential for cottage industries to develop using the abundant resources of *Lantana* to make paper or weave baskets.

'It addresses the problem of keeping an invasive species under control,' says Shonil Bhagwat, Lecturer in Geography at the UK's Open University. 'A concern for conservationists is how to sustain more endemic or endangered species within ecosystems. Keeping *Lantana* within bounds by cutting it back for basketry and so on could provide a win-win solution.'

Colin Clubbe agrees that managing invasives alongside native plants in mixed habitats may be the best way forward, especially as climate change prompts further shifts in plant distributions around the world. And, as it turns out, not all of the Victorian scientists' introductions of foreign species into new habitats have been negative.

Ascension Island's Green Mountain provides a living example of how a collection of non-native plants can form a thriving ecosystem. Today, the mountain is swathed in lush cloud forest that is not indigenous. In fact, the island has only around twenty-five native plant species, ten of which are not found anywhere else.

The story of how the mountain came to be covered in trees dates back to Charles Darwin's voyage on the *Beagle*. In 1836, the ship called for four days at Ascension, which had been settled by the British and used from 1815 as a strategic base for the Royal

Navy (Napoleon was imprisoned on nearby St Helena at the time). After roaming the 'desert Volcanic rocks' of the island, Darwin was struck with the imaginative notion of turning the island into a green oasis – a 'Little England'.

By the time Joseph Hooker, Charles Darwin's friend, arrived on the island for his first visit in 1843, it had become a thriving imperial outpost, the further expansion of which was limited only by a lack of fresh water. By now, Darwin had shared his idea with Hooker, and the two concocted a plan to overcome this difficulty. By establishing trees on Ascension, they aimed to capture rainwater, reduce the high levels of evaporation and create fertile soils. With the enthusiastic help of the Royal Navy, keen to make the island self-sufficient, and of Joseph's father, William at Kew, shipments of plants began to arrive at Ascension from 1850. By the late 1870s, eucalyptus, Norfolk Island pine, bamboo and banana plants were all competing for space on the island's highest peak. Now the imported vegetation captures mist from the surrounding Atlantic Ocean, mitigating the aridity, just as Darwin and Hooker had predicted.

Today, Ascension Island's cloud forest represents a novel ecosystem, comprising a combination of 200–300 non-native and native, invasive and naturalised species. Kew's historic plant introductions essentially represent the world's first experiment in 'terraforming', as they resulted in a self-sustaining ecosystem that helped to make the island more habitable. With the forecasted impacts of climate change looming large, botanists are now beginning to view Green Mountain as an example of how functioning and resilient ecosystems may be 'created' in future, using non-native species. Although extreme invasives will always be viewed as 'the enemy', other non-native plants may have a role to play in supporting ecosystems that include high numbers of indigenous species.

Nonetheless, the struggle faced by Kew and the island's conservationists to bring the parsley fern back from the brink of extinction, and the ongoing efforts to control *Lantana camara* and *Rhododendron ponticum*, demonstrate how difficult it is to strike a balance between the natives and the incomers. With plant species that are new to science still being identified at a rate of 2,000 per year, as yet unknown botanical troublemakers may be poised for invasion. And we have still to discover exactly what it is that makes some plants flourish in locations far from their origins, a conundrum that vexed Charles Darwin back in 1844: 'Many plants seem made to live every where & others no where but where they *seem* to have been generated.' Examining how a balanced ecosystem sprang to life on Ascension Island may help inform our approaches to tackling alien invasive species in the future.

10

PATTERNS FROM CROSSED PEAS

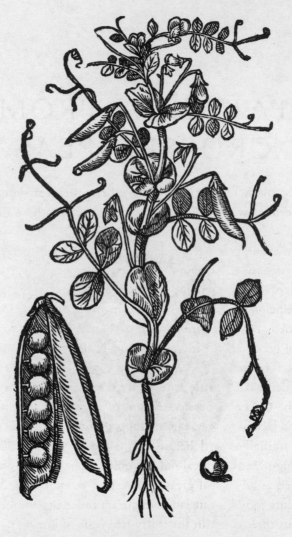

Pea plant, from John Gerard's *Herbal or General Historie of Plantes*, 1633

G REGOR MENDEL COULD have been the great 'might-have-been' of science. A versatile mind, he began his working life as a gardener, trained to become a teacher while practising within an Augustinian monastery, and ended up contributing to scientific fields as diverse as astronomy and meteorology. But his true calling was that of botanist, and today he is revered for unravelling Nature's basic principles of heredity by experimenting on pea plants within his garden. His pioneering work paved the way for the modern study of genetics. But it is only through luck that Mendel's name was not forgotten.

Mendel had to battle hard to have a scientific career since he faced the twin enemies to freedom of scientific thought: lack of time and lack of money. His attempts to make a living as a school-teacher initially failed because he couldn't pass his exams. His most important botanical publication, which would eventually be identified as a work of great importance, was squirrelled away in an obscure journal, but failed to attract much attention, and was cited just three times in the thirty-five years following its publication. Darwin didn't even know of its existence. But when Mendel's ideas did see the light of day they ignited a furious debate, until eventually his insights were tested, completed, extended and accepted as a vital tool in everything from baking bread to controlling disease. The potential nobody of science became the father of modern genetics almost overnight.

Like many iconic figures, the Mendel we know today is part man, part myth. We might picture an obscure, not very well-educated Austrian monk, poring over his pea plants in a monastery garden until the vespers bell summons him to prayer. This image is valid, but only up to a point. Gregor Mendel wasn't Austrian, and he wasn't a monk. He wasn't even called Gregor.

Johann Mendel was born in 1822 into a German family in what is now the Czech Republic, then part of the Austrian Empire. Brought up on a farm, as a young man he worked both as a gardener and a beekeeper. Like a number of leading thinkers and writers of the period, he suffered from ill-health in childhood, missing long periods of formal education, including, on one occasion, an entire year. But in 1840 he entered the University of Olomouc. Although he suffered bouts of depression, he distinguished himself academically in maths and physics and graduated three years later.

Creative tension was significant between the two pillars of wisdom, science and religion in the nineteenth century. Many leading figures of the day had an intellectual foot in both camps: Darwin trained as a Church of England clergyman, for example. Although we have little evidence as to the nature of Mendel's faith, it appears to have formed an enlightened and forward-looking symbiosis with his personal brand of science. Mendel's physics teacher, Friedrich Franz, had suggested the Augustinian career path, so Mendel entered the Abbey of St Thomas, taking the name Gregor. Friars, unlike monks, live and work in the community rather than in a closed monastic house, and Mendel was assigned the appropriate job of teacher in a high school. However, he failed the oral exam, the last of the three exams necessary to gain his teaching certificate. In 1851 his abbot, C.F. Napp, sent him to the University of Vienna to study physics under Christian Doppler (discoverer of the eponymous effect, which explains both why an ambulance siren changes pitch as it whizzes past, and how big the galaxy is). Two years later, Mendel returned to St Thomas's aiming to teach physics but he failed his exam again. In this repeated inability to master the oral part of the exam, we may perhaps see an early example of a brilliant scientific mind struggling with language. In any event, he was given a teaching position at a secondary school in 1867, and eventually he succeeded Napp as abbot.

For all his initial obscurity, Mendel is a good example of how the name of one scientist can become attached to an idea that actually emerged from the simultaneous work of a number of like-minded pioneers. Johann Karl Nestler was Mendel's head of department at the School of Natural History and Agriculture at Olomouc. When Mendel arrived there, Nestler was deeply involved in a series of experiments concerning the hereditary traits of plants and animals. Mendel became interested in how physical and behavioural characteristics are passed on, in the words of one of his daily ration of psalms, *'in generatione et generatione'*: from one generation to another. Nestler and Franz were not his only mentors: Mendel also received considerable encouragement and help from his colleagues at St Thomas's.

Once re-established at the friary, Mendel began to conduct experiments on bees and mice. Both lines of enquiry ran into difficulties for different reasons: a cross-bred population of bees turned out to be so vicious they had to be destroyed, and the bishop objected to one of his underlings studying the sex life of rodents. So Mendel turned to peas.

He observed a variety of traits in pea plants, including height, smoothness of seed and colour. He then cross-pollinated individuals and kept careful records of which characteristics were passed on and how. For example, he crossed plants that produced yellow peas with those producing green. He then replicated the experiment a vast number of times to eliminate the effect of mere chance. When his first generation of hybrids flowered and bore fruit, every pea was yellow. Mendel concluded that there must be three types of pea: pure-breeding yellow; pure-breeding green; and a mixture (the scourge of the hybridist), which, although its peas came out yellow, could still produce green peas in the next generation. Mendel used the concepts for 'dominant' and 'recessive' to explain how parental characteristics were passed on. A plant inherited one version of each characteristic from each of its parents, two in total. If one was dominant and the other recessive, then only the dominant version would show up in the new plant as, for example, the colour of its petals. He wrote up what he had found in a paper published in 1866, which established the laws of inheritance. It was entitled *Experiments in Plant Hybridisation*.

It looked on the face of it as if Mendel's experiments might have shown what plant breeders had known for decades: that behind all the maths, most hybrids return to their parental form. But Mendel had tackled the problem systematically. Thanks to him, science had now established the mathematical laws governing hybridisation, yet it still didn't know how this happened. Mendel knew what had gone on, but couldn't explain its cause.

Once Mendel was elevated to the position of abbot, it largely put an end to his scientific work as he ended up spending all his time on administration and sorting out squabbling colleagues. He got embroiled in an unseemly wrangle with the regional government about the tax affairs of the friary, and after his death his

William Colenso, naturalist-missionary acquaintance of Joseph Hooker, contributed some 6,000 plant specimens from New Zealand to the Kew Herbarium, and also Maori artefacts to its Museum of Economic Botany, including this bottle gourd showing a facial tattoo

The New Zealand flax (*Phormium tenax*), sent back to Kew by Colenso. An economic mainstay plant known as *harakeke* by the Maori, used for textiles and basketry

During William Hooker's Directorship at Kew, his son Joseph undertook extensive travels, first to Antarctica and later to India. He published his findings in *Flora Antarctica* and *Illustrations of Himalayan Plants*, both extensively illustrated by the botanical artist W.H. Fitch with whom he had a long working relationship

Magnolia hodgsonii (previously called *Talauma*) from Joseph Hooker's *Illustrations of Himalayan Plants* (*far left*), and *Anisotome latifolia* from the Auckland and Campbell Islands in *Flora Antarctica*, Vol. 1

Prussian naturalist Alexander von Humboldt spent five years in South America (1799–1804), mapping the way in which temperature changes with altitude and producing some of the first maps that showed distribution ranges of plants

In 1837, when exploring the interior of British Guiana (now Guyana), Robert Schomburgk encountered a huge floating leaf with 'a luxuriant flower' on the river Berbice. It was sent to English botanist John Lindley and named *Victoria regia*, later *Victoria amazonica*, the giant Amazonian waterlily

W.H. Fitch's famous botanical illustrations of the Amazonian waterlily, including the underside of the giant leaf, showing cantilevers radiating from the centre and bracing ribs that give it the strength to bear weight. Joseph Paxton drew on this structure to design a glasshouse for the plant, and to construct the Crystal Palace for the Great Exhibition of 1851.

The flower of the lily which in the wild is pollinated by a beetle, is white on the first evening it opens. When it reopens on the second night it is pink

Orchidmania: Kew botanists coaxed the tropical cockleshell orchid *Prosthechea cochleata* (*left*) to bloom for the first time in 1787. Very soon every botanical enthusiast in Britain was desperate to cultivate these mysterious plants. *Cattleya labiata* (*below*), from Brazil, particularly ignited enthusiasm for orchid collecting

An illustration of *Cattleya skinneri* (now called *Guarianthe skinneri*) from the weighty and lavish tome *The Orchidaceae of Mexico and Guatemala*, by plantsman and garden designer James Bateman

Bateman sent Charles Darwin specimens of *Angraecum sesquipedale* with its astounding foot-long nectar-producing spur. Darwin speculated that there must be a species of moth with a tongue of equal length that fed from it. It was not until 1992 that images were captured to show this

Gregor Mendel observed a variety of traits in pea plants, including flower, seed and pod colour. His carefully documented plant-breeding experiments contributed hugely to understanding of how inherited characteristics are passed from parents to offspring

Rosa gigantea, used by Alister Clark in Australia to create new rose varieties able to tolerate its unforgiving climate, applying knowledge of early geneticists and plant breeders

Books from the library of the Abbey St Thomas, Brno, Czech
Republic, seen here in the Mendel Museum

successor burned all his papers, scientific as well as administrative,
to mark the end of the row.

It would be wrong to think that Mendel died in obscurity,
however. As an abbot he was a figure of some substance. The
young Czech nationalist composer Leos Janáček played the organ
at his funeral. Mendel's scientific writings, too, were well known,
just not those on his studies of inheritance. He had founded the
Austrian Meteorological Society in 1865, and the majority of his
published articles were about the weather. Mendel's paper about
green and yellow peas attracted little attention, however, until the
spring and summer of 1900, sixteen years after his death and
thirty-four years after its publication, when papers by three
botanists unknown to each other, appeared in the same volume
of the *Proceedings of the German Botanical Society*. Hugo de Vries,

Carl Correns and Erich von Tschermak had each independently rediscovered the rules of inheritance that Mendel had identified decades earlier. Mendel's original paper of 1866 may not have attracted much attention, but their papers did. Today, these botanists are credited not only with rescuing Mendel from oblivion, but also with launching the science that would soon come to be called 'genetics'. The century of the gene had begun.

By this time, biology had changed in ways that made Mendel's paper immensely relevant. Mendel had discovered what happened but not how; he had described the effects of inheritance, but couldn't see the mechanics that caused it. In the first decades of the twentieth century, greater scientific understanding of cells and chromosomes (structures present in cells that carry 'genes' or genetic information) gave his ideas a physical reality.

Up to this point, most informed scientific opinion had favoured a 'blending inheritance', where characteristics inherited from each parent would blend in the offspring. But Darwinian theories of evolution required there to be variation for natural selection to work. They also needed some mechanism by which new, unusual and helpful adaptations could be sustained in a wild population. If, sneered the sceptics, the new, useful adaptation was simply watered down, returning to the 'average' character of a large population after the next interbreeding (the logical consequence of 'blending' over several generations), then new varieties and species could never evolve, and Darwinism was wrong. Evolution needed a different model of inheritance. This became known as the 'particulate' theory.

To de Vries, Correns and von Tschermak, Mendel's results proved several things. First, they provided evidence that male and female parents contributed equally to the offspring. This remarkable fact, which we now take for granted, had never been proved before.

Second, they established an understanding of how that parental contribution was passed on.

Mendel's work provided the elegant answer to the tricky question that had intrigued both Darwin and de Vries: how is a newly evolved trait inherited by an offspring and not swamped by the far more prevalent 'average' traits in a population? It was through 'particulate', non-blending inheritance. The concept of dominant and recessive genes has all the beauty and simplicity of the best scientific insights. Once rescued from obscurity, it went on to inform thinking about everything from how to feed developing populations to how to screen for hereditary conditions.

Hugo de Vries, who contributed much to what was to become the science of genetics had known Darwin, and liked him. In his one trip to England (which also took in a tour of Kew and an uncomfortable dinner with Joseph Hooker), he spent the day with the older scientist and they discussed their overlapping areas of interest. This gave de Vries plenty of time to observe Darwin's characteristics.

Darwin has deep set eyes and in addition very protruding eyebrows, much more than one would say from his portrait. He is tall and thin and has thin hands, he walks slowly and uses a cane and has to stop from time to time. He is very much afraid of draughts and generally has to be very careful with his health. His speech is very lively, merry and cordial, not too quick and very clear. It is remarkable how soon one feels at home with people who are friendly and cordial. What a difference with Hooker and Dyer; they were cold and I did not care about them. But I enjoyed my visit with Darwin and I feel much more happy these last days. It is such a pleasure to find that somebody is really interested in you and that he cares about what you have discovered.

De Vries's later work provided a bridge between Darwin's unfinished theories and Mendel's overlooked research.

Another prominent advocate of Mendel's work was the distinguished biologist William Bateson. The story goes that Bateson was on his way to deliver a lecture to the Royal Horticultural Society in London and settled down to read Mendel's paper on the train. Immediately realising its synchronicity with his own ideas, he tore up and rewrote his lecture there and then. In fact the timing of the journey, on 8 May 1900, makes it more likely that he read a paper by de Vries on the train, tracking down Mendel's work only later.

For Bateson, Mendel's work provided exactly what was needed to close an ongoing debate about heredity and the environment. Bateson believed that changes in traits occurred by sudden leaps between one generation and the next (so-called discontinuous variation) rather than gradual changes as proposed by Darwin. Mendel's emphasis on cleanly distinct either/or 'unit' characters – green or yellow; round or wrinkled – was a good match for Bateson's ideas on discontinuous variation. Life might still be a game of chance, but the rules of the game were now an exact science.

Bateson became one of Mendel's most effective champions. His audiences were spellbound. He was clearly an effective communicator and a natural publicist, as shown by the story of the 'eureka' moment on the train, with its whiff of 'spin'. Plant breeders, too, were quick to spot the potential of what Bateson was describing: if preserving the best characteristics of a crop from one generation to another was now science, not luck, then Mendelism could be a powerful tool in maximising output and, therefore, profit.

While Bateson spread the word, Roland Biffen, first Professor of Agricultural Botany at Cambridge, put it into practice. Biffen believed that British farmers could fight back against the so-called

Roland Biffen, pioneer wheat geneticist, in 1926

'grain invasion' from America and Canada if they had access to new, stronger, wheat varieties. Having studied patterns of disease resistance in wheat, he noticed how closely the distribution of disease and resistance followed the classic pattern of Mendelian inheritance. He was convinced he could now replicate this in transferring 'strength' from American to British wheat. Biffen assembled a collection of wheat and barley from all over the world and began his experiments in hybridisation. They worked. As a result of his efforts, grain crops were made less vulnerable to disease, and bread production became more efficient, more profitable and more reliable.

Hybridisation continues to be a powerful tool for gardeners, industrialists, farmers and policy-makers today. It can help with all sorts of problems: tolerance to salinity, resistance to disease, controlling flowering times and improving cropping for fruit trees. Here's just one example: how do you grow roses in an unforgiving climate like that of Australia? Alister Clark set out to create roses capable of withstanding the famously hot, dry Australian summers.

Kew's Director of Horticulture, Richard Barley, describes seeing the results of Clark's efforts when he was a child in the Antipodes: 'He selected things like *Rosa gigantea*, and he bred twenty or thirty of these magnificent rose forms, all named after wives of friends, so they have names like "Marjory Palmer". We had one growing next to our mailbox; it grew like a triffid and had the most ferocious thorns.'

The science of genetics made it possible to control, manipulate and even design plants (and, later, animals). Botany had become botanical science. A further step from building in genetic characteristics by cross-breeding was introducing them artificially in the lab, the process known as genetic modification, or GM. For some, this was (and still is) a step too far. Are we building in potential dangers by circumventing nature's own slow, reliable mechanisms for weeding them out? Or are we simply doing Nature's own job better? The 'century of the gene' has brought its own challenges.

II

TOWARDS THE LIGHT

Pl.2.

Bessa del.   Gabriel Sculp.

BETULA populifolia.

White Birch.

Leaves of a birch tree

WHY DO TREES grow upwards? Some grow a very long way up indeed. In a corner of Kew Gardens, near what is reported to be the biggest compost heap in the world, is a vertiginous but spectacular treetop walk. Climb the stairs to the top of the giant spiders' web of metal mesh and steel stilts, designed to rust into a mellow, autumnal red, and you find yourself among the topmost canopies of some of Kew's finest trees: sweet chestnuts, limes and oaks.

These trees are at work. They spread their leaves gratefully to draw energy direct from the ultimate power supply of all life on earth, the sun. But it is only relatively recently that scientists have worked out how they do it. It turns out that what makes them tall also makes them green.

The key is a biomolecule known as chlorophyll, which allows plants to absorb energy from light (whilst also giving them their green colour). The word was coined in around 1810 from two Greek words, *chloros*, meaning 'pale green', and *phyllon*, meaning 'leaf'. Just over a century later, in 1915, Richard Willstätter earned himself a Nobel Prize (the first ever awarded for Botany) for explaining how it works and what it does.

Plants draw sustenance from above and below. Nutrients and

water come up from the ground through the roots. And food is generated in the leaves via a process whereby water and carbon dioxide are absorbed from the air and converted into glucose and starch, using energy from sunlight and releasing the waste by-product, oxygen, back into the atmosphere. This process is known as photosynthesis.

It's a simple yet vital process, an essential cog in the great interlocking wheel of life on earth. Unravelling its mystery helped draw together an eclectic assortment of scientific loose ends, including answering the question of what the air around us is made of, plus how plants feed themselves and, ultimately, everything else on the planet, including us. It also laid the foundations of twentieth-century plant chemistry.

The ancient Greeks knew that plants draw sustenance from the soil. Like many of their other insights, these ideas were taken up again during the European Renaissance of Classical thought. In the seventeenth century John Ray asked himself how plants can get water to travel upwards, against gravity, and came up with an early prototype of the theory of capillary action. Another naturalist, Stephen Hales (whose day job was vicar of Teddington and who conducted his botanical researches in his spare time), thought sap was analogous to blood in animals and devised experiments to study it. Crucially, Hales became increasingly interested in how plants used water, and was the first to measure how much was given off by the leaves' evaporation. This was a key moment in figuring out what was going on inside the plant's feeding mechanisms.

The ground was now prepared for the principal player in this particular potting shed, Joseph Priestley.

Priestley is a fine example of that uniquely English breed of thinkers and dreamers, a child of his times, a heady amalgam of religious fervour, political radicalism and Enlightenment philosophy, combined with a strong dash of eccentricity and an omnivorous intelligence. His publications include books on grammar, electricity, utilitarian philosophy and Unitarian theology. He was an enthusiast for the French Revolution and, when his house was burned down by an angry mob, fled to rural Pennsylvania, where, undeterred, he founded a new community dedicated to God and truth.

As we have learned, many leading men of science in history were professional divines. Priestley was a Dissenting (that is, non Church of England) clergyman. He had nearly died when he was around fifteen, leaving him with a permanent stutter and a profoundly probing attitude towards matters of faith and doctrine. His aunt, with whom he lived, had always intended him for the ministry (he could recite all 107 questions and answers of the Catechism by heart at the age of four). However, his illness forced a hiatus in his formal studies, into which he crammed every possible kind of reading and learning, including philosophy, metaphysics and languages (French, Italian, German, Chaldean, Syrian and Arabic).

Priestley's principal contribution to the understanding of botanical science was his insight that the atmosphere around us is composed of different 'airs'. He regarded these as varying states of the same thing, rather than separate gases, but the idea led him to conduct a number of experiments into how and when the different states existed and interacted, which provided important insights into the chemical and biological processes of plants.

His system of classification led him to describe a number of different kinds of air, most famously 'dephlogisticated air', or what would later be called oxygen. He demonstrated that this air allowed an animal such as a mouse to breathe, whereas air that had been 'injured' by,

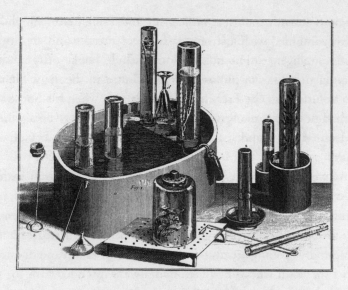

Experimental apparatus from Joseph Priestley's *Experiments and Observations on Different Kinds of Air*, 1774–7

for example, the presence of flame, did not. He also noted that 'injured' air could be restored by the leaves of plants (mint, in his case), which removed the harmful 'phlogiston' from the air.

As always, his work was continued and extended by other scientists. The Frenchman Antoine Lavoisier demonstrated that Priestley's 'dephlogisticated air' was not air from which something had been removed, but was in fact a separate element to which he gave the name 'oxygen', a step that marked a revolution in our understanding of chemistry. Jan Ingenhousz of Breda in Holland linked plants and air more closely in his work 'Experiments upon Vegetables' (which included the observations that plants 'breathe' solely during the day, and that only the green parts do so at all). Finally, a Swiss chemist called Nicolas-Théodore de Saussure did all the precise measurements.

Science now had an explanation for 'why plants grow upwards', which was clear, workable, and capable of repeated proof.

Developments in microscope technology and in the understanding of the cell allowed nineteenth-century experimentalists such as Julius von Sachs to examine the internal structure of plants in ever greater detail. Sachs observed the green structures within cells, called chloroplasts, and the pigment that colours them, chlorophyll, which had first been isolated in 1817. In 1862, Sachs demonstrated that chlorophyll was involved in the production within the cell of tiny starch grains, which the plant then used as food. These grains were not only essential but were produced nowhere else. The importance of the process was becoming clear, together with some of its mechanics: how and where the plant took in water and gases, where it made use of them, and what for.

Sachs's seminal publication, *Text Book of Botany: Morphological and Physiological*, was translated into English from its original German in 1875 by the then Assistant Director of Kew Gardens, William Thiselton-Dyer. It contained the celebrated formula memorised by generations of schoolchildren ever since:

carbon dioxide + water (+ light energy) = glucose + oxygen

Two decades later, in 1897, on the other side of the Atlantic in America, a couple of plant scientists called Charles Barnes and Conway MacMillan gave the process its name: photosynthesis.

Twentieth-century science brought its new skills to bear on the subject. Robin Hill drew on his early work on haemoglobin in blood to look at plant pigments at the level of the atom and the electron. Melvin Calvin investigated how plants stored and used their light-derived energy once the light source had been switched off, and he invented the term 'Calvin–Benson' cycle to describe how they make essential and complex molecules such as cellulose and amino acids.

Later work discovered that plants in dissimilar environments have different photosynthetic pathways. Most plants use the 'C3' pathway. Plants in hot, dry environments like savannahs, however, use either 'C4' or Crassulacean Acid Metabolism (CAM) as their pathway of choice.

'C4' – so-called because the first product of photosynthesis has four carbon atoms rather than the usual three – uses carbon dioxide and, more importantly, water more efficiently, making it advantageous to plants in hot, dry environments. Many savannah plants, which live in semi-arid to semi-humid climes, have a C4 pathway, as do some important food crops such as maize and sugar cane.

In contrast, the pineapple, along with other plants in extremely arid environments (such as cacti), use the CAM mechanism. In CAM plants, the uptake of carbon dioxide from the atmosphere occurs at night. This is because in areas of extreme heat and aridity, cooler night-time temperatures allow the pores in a leaf to be open and gases to enter without the risk of losing large amounts of water through evaporation. During the day the pores are closed.

The night-time absorption of carbon dioxide results in four-carbon organic molecules being formed. The four-carbon molecules are stored in cells capable of undertaking photosynthesis. In daylight hours these stored molecules release their reserves of carbon dioxide, which are fed into the chloroplasts where photosynthesis takes place. These CAM plants, therefore, get their carbon dioxide and their sunlight separately, at different times, not simultaneously like most other plants. This means they have had to develop a way of storing their carbon dioxide as an intermediary molecule until the sun comes up and they can start to use it to make food.

As usual, it took generations of radical scientific thinkers and

Plants that live in extremely arid environments, such as this saguaro cactus in Arizona, take up carbon dioxide at night

experimenters – worrying away at their own pet theories, sometimes working together, but more often in competition – to figure out how photosynthesis works and how it keeps the entire symphony of life on earth all playing together in the same key. Plants treat our atmosphere to its daily detox, its dry-clean, its dose of dephlogistication, and constantly replenish it with oxygen. And next time you saunter along the walkway among the treetops of Kew, you'll be watching them do it.

12

MULTIPLE GENES

MUSA PARADISIACA. L.

The banana, a polyploid plant, the fruit of which was savoured
by Charles Darwin

JOSEPH HOOKER ONCE sent Charles Darwin some bananas from the hothouse at Kew. 'You have not only rejoiced my soul, but my stomach,' replied the great man, 'for the bananas are simply delicious. I never saw any like them.' Jim Endersby sheds some light on Darwin's delight: 'His doctor had forbidden him sugar.' So, in sending the fruit, Hooker was doing a double good turn to 'his sweet-toothed friend'.

Bananas were, at this time, exotic rarities. Encouraged by demand for their honeyed flavour, horticulturalists began to cultivate them but found they could only do so by taking cuttings, essentially cloning them. This meant the plants they generated were all genetically identical to their parent, leaving them vulnerable to exploitation by pests and diseases. The conundrum presented science with the challenge of understanding how such a large cultivated population could be sustained, and what the potential threats to its survival were.

As it happened, efforts to provide us with bananas, now the world's most popular fruit, led to a growing understanding of one of the key processes by which plants have evolved over millions of years. The process in question seems, initially at least, a strange occurrence. And it has an appropriately strange name:

polyploidy. But understanding this process has been fundamental to helping botanists develop new approaches to cultivating and protecting key global crops, including wheat, cotton, potato and sugar cane.

The word polyploidy means 'many forms', and refers to a phenomenon by which plants acquire multiple sets of chromosomes (structures made of DNA that carry genetic information, or genes) within their cells. This is courtesy of a beneficial kink in the process of reproduction. Typically, a plant's reproductive cells – ova and pollen – undergo a process known as meiosis during reproduction in which the number of sets of chromosomes in each cell is halved from two (diploid) to one (haploid). When these cells fuse together during fertilisation, they create a new plant in which the original number of chromosomes is restored – basically, 1 + 1 = 2.

Polyploidy is what you get when this process takes a different path. Rather than a plant producing reproductive cells containing just one set of chromosomes each, sometimes twin-set versions are thrown into the mix. This arises from a failure in meiosis. If a diploid cell fuses with a haploid cell, the resulting plant will have three chromosome sets (2 + 1) rather than two, creating a triploid plant – a category that includes some varieties of apple as well as the world's main commercial variety of banana.

Likewise, if the plant cells that fuse are both diploid, the simple arithmetic of 2 + 2 creates a new hybrid plant with four sets of chromosomes in each cell, known as a tetraploid. A plant with four sets of chromosomes can breed with a twin-set diploid to produce a plant with six sets of chromosomes per cell. Bread wheat is one of those, known as a hexaploid. Certain varieties of strawberry, meanwhile, are decaploids, containing cells with ten sets of chromosomes.

The highest ploidy level so far recorded in a flowering plant is found in a stonecrop (*Sedum*) from Mexico with eighty sets of chromosomes in each cell, while a species of the adder's tongue fern (*Ophioglossum*) is the record-holder for the entire plant kingdom – a ninety-six-ploid wonder. 'Plants are very diverse in terms of polyploidy,' says Kew plant geneticist Ilia Leitch, 'in contrast to mammals, which are all reported to be diploid.'

Mammals should perhaps count their luck. Triploid plants can't reproduce sexually (but they can reproduce vegetatively by producing clones); neither can any plant with an odd number of chromosome sets. This is because you can't split an odd number in two during meiosis to provide the whole number of chromosomes needed to produce fertile reproductive cells. That's why, when you peel a modern banana, you won't find any seeds inside – as you would if you went back thousands of years and peeled one of its wild ancestors. It also explains why growers have had to take an asexual path, propagating from grafts, to breed the banana and other triploid plants.

But polyploidy also provides a way out of the infertility cul-de-sac faced by some of the sterile hybrids it creates. If another round of polyploidal activity further doubles the number of chromosomes, you get a new hybrid with an even number of chromosomes (such as 3 + 3 = 6). This new hybrid will then be able to undergo normal meiosis and breed sexually. This ability for polyploidy to free hybrid plants from infertility has proved to be crucial for key crops such as maize.

Rather than being Frankenstein creations fit only to skulk at the edge of Nature, plants that result from polyploidy are sufficiently widespread for botanists to believe the process provides some sort of evolutionary trump card. Kew scientists have contributed to discovering and analysing some of the benefits it provides, which include an influence on growth speed, fruit size, height and soil tolerance, as well as resistance to drought, pests and disease.

The early stirrings of polyploidy research began in 1890, when the Dutch plant biologist and Mendel supporter Hugo de Vries spotted an intriguing cluster of *Oenothera lamarckiana* (evening primrose of Lamarck) that had escaped from a garden and established itself on an abandoned potato field near the Dutch town of Hilversum. The plants varied greatly in their size. It was hard to miss, according to de Vries, 'attracting immediate attention, even from a distance'. For him, this chance discovery provided the evidence he was looking for that Charles Darwin was wrong. Rather than accepting the Darwinian thesis that evolution proceeded gradually by the natural selection of small variations over long periods of time, de Vries believed that significant evolutionary change could be driven by larger variations over short periods.

When de Vries took seeds from the Hilversum plants, he discovered that they produced further variants that were distinct from the parent plant, in a process he called spontaneous mutation. This was the first use of the term in genetics, which de Vries cemented with the publication of his two-volume book *The Mutation Theory* (1900–1903).

Around the time de Vries was preparing to publish the first volume of his book, another intriguing example of polyploidy was offered up at Kew. Gardener Frank Garrett noticed a mysterious primula hybrid among the seedlings in one of the Gardens' greenhouses. The new plant, which came as a surprise to everyone at Kew, appeared to be a novel offspring of the buttercup primrose (*Primula floribunda*) – a native of the Himalaya – and *Primula verticillata*, a plant hailing from the very different climes of Arabia. Because of its location, the newcomer was christened *Primula* × *kewensis* and its spectacular flowers saw it scoop a First Class Certificate at the Royal Horticultural Society's 1900 meeting.

The prizewinning *Primula* × *kewensis*

But this first plant turned out to be a sterile hybrid. So did all the further plants Garrett and his team produced by crossing the two parental species, much to their frustration. Then, in 1905, one branch of one plant miraculously produced a few fertile flowers, whose seeds gave rise to a fertile giant form of the Kew primula. This enigmatic release from infertility attracted the interest of botanist Lettice Digby, who counted the chromosomes in both the sterile and fertile versions of the plant. Her conclusion: the fertile one owed its fertility to a polyploidal doubling in its number of chromosomes.

Further research gradually revealed that many key crop plants were polyploidal. Research into the phenomenon gathered pace. But, as commercial interest united with science, the limits of research became apparent. While researchers were able to count chromosomes easily enough, they were not yet able to artificially induce polyploidy in the laboratory so that its practical potential could be explored. This was the polyploidal Holy Grail.

Success was achieved in the late 1930s, when US researchers Albert Francis Blakeslee and Amos Greer Avery isolated a chemical that promoted chromosome doubling in plants: colchicine. It comes from the autumn crocus (*Colchicum autumnale*, sometimes known as meadow saffron), which was known to have been used to treat rheumatic complaints as far back as 1500 BC, when it was mentioned in the Ebers Papyrus, the oldest surviving Egyptian medical text.

The methods used to count chromosomes in plant cells were – and, in many laboratories, remain – time-consuming, involving squashing small amounts of plant root, and staining them to show their chromosomes, which then can be counted under a microscope.

More recently, Kew scientists have turned to flow cytometry to study polyploidy. In this method, cells are suspended in a stream of fluid and zapped by a laser to analyse the physical and chemical

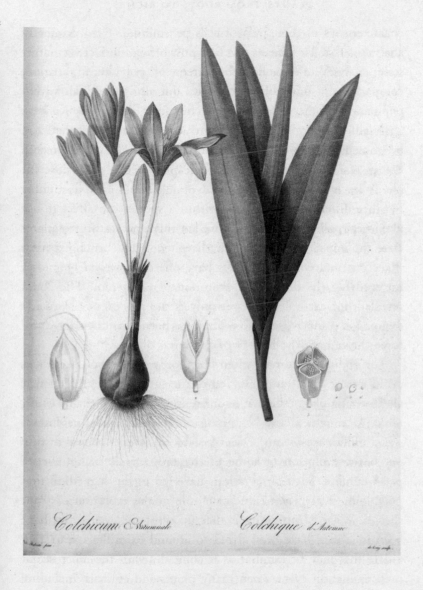

Colchicum Autumnale   *Colchique d'Automne*

The autumn crocus, original source of colchicine, which
promotes chromosome doubling in plants

characteristics of thousands of cells per minute. Flow cytometry analysis is fast. This means it is now possible to conduct very large-scale analyses to establish the extent of polyploidy variation, comparing not only different species but also individuals within populations of the same species. Such studies, some of which have analysed over 5,000 individual plants, have revealed that there can be immense ploidal variation within a species. The current record holder is a species of ragweed (*Senecio*) in which eight different ploidy levels have been identified.

Since different ploidy levels within a species can affect things like insect pollinator behaviour, we are only now starting to appreciate the impact of such genetic diversity, as Ilia Leitch explains: 'Recently, molecular techniques have offered powerful new tools for studying the origin and evolution of polyploids. They have revealed, for example, that not only is the process of polyploidy ongoing in plants we see today, but it has been a major evolutionary force throughout the history of flowering plants.'

The ability to estimate when polyploidy events took place over evolutionary time frames has led to the surprising revelation that all flowering plants share at least one such common event, which took place right at the beginning of flowering plant evolution, *c.*200 million years ago. Other polyploidy events occurred early on in the evolution of some of the most species-rich (diverse) plant families. Such observations have led to the suggestion that polyploidy may play a significant role in the evolution of plant species. What is intriguing is that many of the events that have been identified have been dated to around 65 million years ago, a date that may be familiar as it coincides with the most recent mass extinction event when many plants and animals, including the dinosaurs, went extinct. Perhaps polyploids were better able to survive compared with their diploid relatives.

Why does this matter? Is our understanding of polyploidy simply a question of pure research, or does it have any practical applications? 'We have sequenced the DNA from enough plants to see a general pattern emerging,' says Kew's Mark Chase. In plants that have undergone multiple polyploidy events during their evolution, particular genes that control other 'structural' genes (which determine the way a plant looks and acts), are retained in many copies. These controlling genes have become known as 'transcription factors'. Kew scientists believe they provide a key to unlocking the benefits conferred by polyploidy. 'Because there are multiple transcription factors controlling the structural genes in polyploidal plants, they can respond to the environment in much more complicated ways than plants in which there are fewer transcription factors,' continues Chase.

One area where understanding of polyploidy and transcription factors can be applied is in protecting crops from disease, which brings us back to where we started: bananas. Not only are bananas the cornerstone of many emerging economies, but they are our planet's fourth most important staple food after rice, wheat and maize. We can't afford to let the genetically lean banana become a rarity again through disease. Luckily, understanding polyploidy could help it avoid that fate.

Virtually all bananas traded internationally are a single variety, Cavendish, with distant genetic roots in India. But in recent years the Cavendish has been under attack from a number of fungal diseases, including Black Sigatoka, as deadly to bananas as the blight that destroyed Ireland's potatoes in the nineteenth century. In the Caribbean, this single fungus has already ravaged banana plantations covering 70 per cent of the arable land and employing three quarters of the working population in places such as St Vincent and the Grenadines. Some islands have seen their banana exports plummet by 80 per cent. Others can no longer export at all.

A particular weak point of the Cavendish is that it is one of those triploid mutants, whose cropping bounty has come at the expense of its fertility. Evidence suggests that the growers' need to use grafting for reproduction has helped transmit fungal diseases from generation to generation. So labs across the world are deploying our understanding of polyploidy and hybridisation to try to create alternatives to the Cavendish that match it for taste and durability, while offering disease resistance.

Particular hope is being pinned on research in the banana's ancestral genetic homeland of India, where the continuing diversity of banana types provides a hugely valuable gene resource. India's National Research Centre for Banana has already evaluated over 1,000 types – including wild species – in its search for ones with natural resistance to Black Sigatoka and other diseases.

Darwin's doctor was right. It's much better for us to eat bananas than sugar. If scientists can use their understanding of polyploidy to help improve crops, we will all be able to carry on eating bananas and, like Darwin, rejoicing in both soul and stomach at the continued abundance of this nutritious and economically significant fruit.

13

BATTLING BARK AND BEETLE

Wych elms killed by Dutch elm disease in Scotland in 2007

I N LONDON'S NATIONAL Gallery hangs one of the nation's
favourite paintings. *The Hay Wain*, painted by John Constable
in 1821, depicts a peaceful rural scene of a wagon crossing a stream
that flows alongside a row of elegant elm trees. When Constable
painted it, partly from his London studio, he was well aware that
the urbanisation and transportation that had been unleashed by
the industrial revolution were about to change England's predom-
inantly agricultural way of life for ever. What Constable could not
have known, however, was that the increased movement of people
and products would also alter the English countryside in a wholly
unpredictable way.

His painting shows an iconic English treescape that no one
born after 1970 would be able to recognise, because the countryside Constable knew was full of elm trees growing in prominent,
dense stands. The botanist Henry Elwes wrote of the elm: 'Its true
value as a landscape tree may be best estimated by looking down
from an eminence in almost any part of the valley of the Thames,
or of the Severn below Worcester, during the latter half of November,
when the bright golden colour of the lines of elms in the hedge-
rows is one of the most striking scenes that England can produce.'

But by the time he had penned these words, a fungus, distributed by a beetle, was already destroying Europe's elm population. The billowing elm crowns that Elwes had loved and Constable had captured so well were soon to disappear from the countryside for good.

The disease was not spotted until 1918, by which time it was already well established across Belgium, the Netherlands and parts of northern France. It was first seen in Britain in 1927. Controversy raged about its potential causes, among those put forward being drought, gas poisoning from the First World War, a bacterium and a variation of *Nectria* canker disease. The real culprit was eventually uncovered by the painstaking work, between 1919 and 1934, of seven Dutch women scientists, all of whom had studied at the Willie Commelin Scholten Phytopathology Laboratory, near Utrecht. One of Europe's leading centres for the study of plant diseases, the laboratory was remarkable for its predominance of outstanding female scientists.

It was graduate student Bea Schwarz who identified that the fungus *Graphium ulmi* (now called *Ophiostoma ulmi*) was killing the trees, but very few people believed her. It was not until her colleague Christine Buisman repeated and expanded Schwarz's experiments that the original studies were vindicated. The women scientists had identified the cause, and the malady (perhaps rather unfairly) took its name from their nationality: Dutch elm disease. However, whilst Schwarz and Buisman had provided vital information about the cause of the devastation, unfortunately they couldn't provide a cure.

By the 1940s, the fungus had killed between 10 and 40 per cent of the elms in several European countries but then for a time it seemed to die down. Tom Peace, who monitored the spread of the disease across the UK on behalf of the Forestry Commission, wrote in 1960 (with what turned out to be misplaced confidence): 'Unless it completely changes its present trend of behaviour it will never bring about the disaster once considered imminent.'

That change soon materialised. In the late 1960s, the fungus was superseded by a more aggressive pathogen, *Ophiostoma novo-ulmi*, which made its way into Britain via infested elm logs imported for boat-building. Carried by two beetle compatriots, the European elm bark beetle (*Scolytus multistriatus*) and the large elm bark beetle (*S. scolytus*), it began a fast-paced march across the countryside, particularly favouring the English elm (*Ulmus procera*). Attracted to stressed, dying or dead elm wood, the beetles tunnelled into the bark and formed galleries in which they laid their eggs. When these hatched, the larvae fed off the inner bark and sapwood. If the tree was already infected with the fungus, it produced sticky spores in the larval galleries. Then, when the larvae emerged as adult beetles, they carried these spores with them on to healthy trees, on which they fed. Within a decade, two thirds of Britain's 30 million elms were lost.

Tony Kirkham, Head of Kew's Arboretum, explains that the disease moves around through xylem cells – the tissue that transports water, and sometimes nutrients, from the roots to the elm's superstructure. In an attempt to stop the disease, trees block the xylem cells, cutting off their own water supplies – in effect, committing suicide. This brings about a very quick death; from the moment that they succumb to the disease to their dying takes about a year.

Kirkham recalls witnessing the impact of Dutch elm disease at Kew Gardens in the late 1970s. While attending lectures as a horticultural diploma student, he saw the Gardens' last elms being felled as he looked out of the classroom window. 'Before the disease appeared, the dominant trees in the Gardens were elm, oak and beech,' he says. 'But we lost the entire elm collection apart from

The field, *or common English,* Elm.

Full-grown tree in Kensington Gardens, 65 ft. high ; diam. of the trunk 3 ft., and of the head 48 ft.
[Scale 1 in. to 12 ft.]

The common English elm, from J.C. Loudon's
The Trees and Shrubs of Britain, 1838

one or two species, so I never saw mature elms growing at Kew. The treescape changed overnight, as elms were lost across the entire country.'

Trees affected by the disease are easy to spot as, when their internal water supply is switched off, their leaves wilt, becoming yellow and brown in early summer, then falling off. The affected shoots die back from the tip, sometimes turning down into a distinctive 'shepherd's crook' shape. Peeling back the bark on live shoots of diseased trees reveals brown or purple longitudinal streaks. Elms are not usually susceptible until they reach maturity, when they are around fifteen to twenty years old. Only at that age does the bark change to form a habitat in which the *Scolytus* beetles can complete their life cycles.

Interestingly, analyses of fossil pollen that have been conducted on sediment cores taken from lakes and bogs show that a similar major decline in the number of elm trees took place across north-western Europe around 6,000 years ago. This roughly coincides with the beginnings of Neolithic farming, leading to much debate as to whether the elm decline was caused by the first farmers cutting down trees to clear land, or whether this was an early outbreak of Dutch elm disease. Pollen evidence gathered at Diss Meer, in Norfolk, for example, shows that the elm decline in that region took only six years. This rapid impact is consistent with the effects of a disorder such as Dutch elm disease, yet no evidence of the fungus responsible was found in the Norfolk sediments.

However, later discoveries of remains of the *Scolytus scolytus* beetle in Neolithic deposits from Hampstead Heath in London certainly suggest that the disease was present in the UK at that time. And wood showing the characteristic galleries made by the beetles has now been found at Neolithic sites in Switzerland and Denmark. The disease is therefore nothing new – but it is only

Larval galleries of the elm bark beetle, which spreads the
disease-causing fungus *Ophiostoma novo-ulmi*

in the past 100 years or so that we have recorded its impacts and
witnessed their significance.

Up until the early 1970s, Dutch elm disease had been the only
major blight affecting trees in the UK but fresh threats have
since emerged. In 2012, Clive Brasier, Emeritus Mycologist at
Forest Research, the Forestry Commission's research agency,
charted new outbreaks of diseases that had affected trees or
the natural environment in the UK between 1970 and 2012. The
graph showed that, until 1994, Dutch elm disease was the only
major infection recorded. However, from that date onwards, it
revealed a massive increase in numbers, as other trees – including
alder, pine, beech, horse chestnut, hornbeam, native heath, larch,
Lawson's cypress, native juniper, sweet chestnut and ash – con-
secutively succumbed to an array of diseases, many caused by

species of *Phytophthora* (water moulds of the same kind that causes late blight in potatoes).

Two possible culprits for the sudden rise are increasing climatic variability resulting from climate change, and the ease of movement of people (and plants) across borders. But are there practical ways to mitigate the spread of such diseases? Although the issue is high on the agenda, it may be too late to prevent even more invasions. 'There are a lot of pests and diseases out there still waiting to come into this country that we don't really want,' explains Kirkham. 'Asian longhorn beetle, citrus longhorn beetle, emerald ash bore: we haven't got these yet on a large scale but when we've had a few instances of them, we've managed to eradicate them. Pine processionary moth is just waiting around the corner. We need to be ready so that when these things do come, we can react fast and eradicate them. Once they're in the country, it's often too late, so prevention is better than cure.'

The latest disease to hitch a ride on incoming nursery stocks is ash dieback, caused by the fungus *Hymenoscyphus pseudoalbidus*. Trees were first reported to be dying from the disease in Poland in 1992. From there it began spreading across Europe, arriving in the UK in 2012, when a consignment of infected trees was sent from a nursery in the Netherlands to one in Buckinghamshire. As of May 2014, it had been found at 646 sites in the UK, covering Norfolk, Suffolk, south-west Wales and the east coasts of England and Scotland. The disease particularly targets the common or European ash (*Fraxinus excelsior*) and the narrow-leaved ash (*Fraxinus angustifolia*). Usually fatal, it causes leaves to drop and the crown to die back, hence its name.

Mindful of the devastation caused by Dutch elm disease, a UK taskforce has been set up to address this problem. It has suggested a number of initiatives, including a plant passport

Fráxinus excélsior.
The taller, *or common*, Ash.

Full-grown tree in Kensington Gardens, 75 ft. high ; diam. of trunk 4 ft. 6 in., of head 48 ft.
[Scale 1 in. to 12 ft.]

The common European ash, victim of ash dieback, caused by
the fungus *Hymenoscyphus pseudoalbidus*

scheme and better sharing of 'epidemiological intelligence' across the EU, so that past behaviour of plant diseases can be used to inform current and future outbreaks. Part of the solution could also come from Kew's Millennium Seed Bank Partnership (MSBP) at Wakehurst Place, Kew's country estate in West Sussex. Its scientists are on a mission to pinpoint trees with genes that offer natural resistance to ash dieback. They are collecting seeds from specimens in twenty-four zones across the UK, which are known to be genetically different from one another, to create a bank of them for research.

Paul Smith, Director of the MSBP, explains: 'We know that some natural populations of ash in mainland Europe have been identified as having natural resistance. There are groups currently working on trying to understand what the genetic base of that resistance is. Once we've isolated the genes that are responsible, it should be possible to design a very simple genetic test that will enable us to apply it to each seed in the bank. If we find natural resistance there, we have the exact information about where that seed was collected and from which precise tree. We can then go back to the mother tree, collect more seeds and use those to reintroduce ash into the landscape once more.'

Unlike ash trees, which usually grow from seeds, elms tend to be propagated from root cuttings, producing clones that are genetically identical. That is why, when Dutch elm disease arrived, it affected Europe's trees so widely. 'Every elm in a hedgerow for miles and miles and miles through a county was the same clone,' says Tony Kirkham. 'So when the first tree in a stand went, the end one was going to follow suit. It was just a matter of how quickly.'

There is one elm at Kew that was planted in 1905: a Caucasian elm (*Zelkova carpinifolia*), which is known to be resistant to Dutch elm disease. Most of the other elms growing in the Gardens have been planted relatively recently and are thought to have some resistance to it. One of Kew's original specimens of the Himalayan elm (*Ulmus villosa*) ironically survived the disease, only to be felled by the hurricane of 1987 (other impacts of the hurricane are explained in Chapter 18). Luckily, Kirkham's team were able to propagate hardwood cuttings from it with which he replaced the lost tree. He has also planted the Chinese elm (*Ulmus parviflora*), Plot's elm (*Ulmus minor* subspecies *plotii*) and *Ulmus americana* 'Princeton'. Unfortunately the Asian elms are considered less decorative by some than the susceptible British species.

A slender hope that Britain's native elms may yet resist the disease has come from Paul King of King and Co., the tree nursery, which in the 1980s took cuttings from four elm trees that appeared to have survived its ravages. Likely to be a combination of *Ulmus glabra* (the Scots elm), *U. procera* and *U. carpinifolia* (the European elm), these are now two decades old and still going strong. Whether they will make it to full maturity remains to be seen. If they do, we may yet see the elm woodlands of Constable's day returning to the English countryside.

14

HUNT FOR DIVERSITY

Soviet Russian poster, 'Remember those who Starve!'

As HUMANS HAVE moved across the globe we've taken plant life with us. Seeds are small, resilient and easy to carry, and colonists and invaders have taken their native crop plants all over the world. It is now often difficult to know where and when the original, wild ancestors of many of our domesticated plants first evolved. But we can get on their trail by looking at where their wild relatives grow today. The pioneer in this field was a botanist and crop breeder, a man who saw the best of science and the worst of humanity: Nikolai Vavilov.

Born in 1887, Vavilov grew up in the small village of Ivashkovo, close to Moscow. Under the autocratic and inefficient regime of the tsars, crop failures were frequent, and the hardship and famine Vavilov witnessed as a child gave him the lifelong determination to ensure they never happened again. He resolved to use the emerging scientific disciplines of botany and genetics to put an end to such suffering. The appalling irony of Vavilov's work is that whilst he saved others, he could not save himself.

At a time when most botanists were concerned only with wild species, Vavilov set out to uncover the taxonomy of cultivated plants. By undertaking extensive collecting expeditions, he developed a theory about where the wild forebears of today's crops were first taken into cultivation. A supporter of the ideas of Gregor Mendel, he believed that identifying and studying the wild ancestors of modern crop plants would enable botanists to develop new disease-resistant crop cultivars (plant varieties produced commercially by selective breeding) that would help feed the planet. His pioneering work, conducted against a backdrop of revolution and war, alerted the world to the importance of genetic diversity in plants.

Humans began abandoning their hunter-gatherer lifestyle in favour of agriculture as far back as 12,000 years ago. Early farmers selected plants displaying beneficial traits, such as seeds that ripened uniformly and fruits that were juicy and plentiful. And over time, the development of overland trading networks and improved maritime technology enabled them to move their seeds from one continent to another, transforming the globe from a world of foragers to one of farmers. This is why it is difficult to know where and when the wild antecedents of many of our domesticated crops evolved.

You might wonder why this is important, given that we now employ many highly sophisticated farming methods. The answer lies in genetic diversity. In the process of taking wild plants into cultivation, and the subsequent millennia of selection by farmers, genes that confer useful properties – such as resisting disease and coping with climatic variability – have been lost in favour of those that provide high yields and great taste. We now have reliable supplies of better quality food but dangerously reduced genetic variety. Genetically similar crops can be susceptible to pests and diseases – a weakness that has been tragically proven more than once in the course of human history.

In recent times we have embraced 'monoculture' farming: planting vast areas with a few modern cultivars, resulting in high yields but extremely low genetic diversity. Faced with a growing global population, climate change and resulting water scarcity, plant breeders of future crops need access to an array of genes to make plants resilient to more variable environmental conditions than they may have endured in the past. But the only way we can breed crops containing those genes is to find where their wild ancestors live today and tap into their diverse gene pools. This is critically important, given that we rely on just three of the world's 50,000 edible plants (rice, maize and wheat) to provide 60 per cent of our food energy intake. If a pest or disease affects one of these staples, widespread hunger becomes a very real possibility.

Nikolai Vavilov was one of the first scientists to understand that the wild relatives of crops represent important, possibly unique pools of genetic variability that could help successful and sustainable plant breeding for human use. In the early twentieth century, he set out to test his ideas by collecting and studying plants in their wild habitats, undertaking more than 115 research expeditions to sixty-four countries, including Ethiopia, Italy, Kazakhstan, Mexico, Brazil and the USA. He deliberately chose the areas in which agriculture originated, with the specific aim of finding useful genes for crops, both in their wild relatives and in traditional land races selectively grown by farmers.

Vavilov set out his thinking in a letter explaining the need for a plant-collecting trip to Asia Minor (modern-day Turkey).

In nature there is a gigantic store of varieties, as yet unused in the world agricultural industry. For instance, numerous forms of field plants (which the science and practice of the developed countries have been unaware of) in the regions of south-western Asia, western Asia and the Transcaucasus. Cereal grasses of Asia and the Transcaucasus are of great interest from a practical point of view. They are characterised by non-shattering, drought resistance, excellent vitreous grain, tolerance to soil quality, and immunity to many parasitic fungi.

Vavilov used the knowledge he gained on these expeditions to develop his belief that each type of cultivated plant originated from a particular place where the greatest variation in that crop could still be found. He called these places centres of origin.

In 1926 he published the paper *The Centres of Origin of Cultivated Plants*, identifying five major foci of the main field, garden and orchard crops. He noted that these areas were not, as might be expected, concentrated around the great rivers of the world, beside which agriculture was thought to have first been practised and civilised societies had developed, but in the 'mountain areas of Asia (Himalaya and its system), the mountain systems of northeastern Africa and the mountain areas of southern Europe (the Pyrenees, the Apennines and the Balkans), the Cordilleras and the southern spurs of the Rocky Mountains. In the old world the original areas of cultivated plants belong mostly within a belt between 20° and 40° N latitude.'

Today, tucked behind the door of Wing D of Kew's Herbarium, stands a wooden display case, the modest appearance of which belies the importance of its contents. Inside, organised in black box files, is a collection of the ears of 1,300 types of wheat, assembled by the agriculturalist John Percival, which was consulted by Vavilov in his studies. It is clear from the collection, incorporating species and land races, that traditional farmers created an astonishing array of cultivated wheat types. It remains an invaluable resource for scientists working on the effects of agricultural practice on appearance and diversity.

Ears of emmer wheat showing their diversity,
from the Percival Collection

Kew's Mark Nesbitt points to a selection of sheets, each containing several ears of wheat.

You can see that some of these have awns, some don't; some are red, some white, some are black; some are hairy, some are not hairy; some ears are long, some ears are short. What you're seeing is both diversity at the field level of traditional wheat varieties – there's enormous variability just in one farmer's field – but also variability between different species. So there are small-eared wild wheats, emmer wheats from Ethiopia and elsewhere, durum wheats and bread wheats – which are by far the most important wheats today. All of this variation and appearance in morphology reflects underlying genetic variability: things like resistance to disease, culinary properties and the ability to grow on poor soils. For traditional farmers, these are really useful properties.

Nesbitt explains that when farmers began domesticating wheat, only certain plants from the extensive stands of its wild antecedents would have been taken into cultivation. This produced a 'bottleneck' effect, in that the subsequent wheats they farmed contained merely some, rather than all, of the genetic diversity that existed in the plant's wild ancestors. So genetic diversity began to be lost from the moment that we domesticated plants. At the same time, as the Percival wheat collection shows, traditional farmers introduced new variability through seed selection and exchange. However, modern-day cultivars, produced by breeders, have the least genetic diversity of all, as they have been selectively bred to produce uniform crops, making them deficient in genes that might allow them to adapt to extreme drought or other climatic variability.

Dorian Fuller, Professor of Archaeobotany at University College London, takes up the thread:

One of the problems that Vavilov saw in the beginning was that famines were partly caused by large-scale reliance on fewer varieties. He felt that if you could harness some of the variety among species that was out there in the mountainous regions, and in what he called these 'centres of origin', you could find a wider set of genetic diversity that would provide the tools for building in resistance to unknown pressures in the future.

Historical events would have a major impact on Vavilov's work. In the Russian Revolution of 1917, Lenin had gained power.

Bread wheats of the kind bred by Roland Biffen,
from the Percival Collection

Although he hated the intelligentsia, he realised that the country
needed the specialists who worked in its institutes and research
labs, many of which were located in Petrograd (the new name for
St Petersburg between 1914 and 1924), the cradle of the revolution.
Thus it was that in 1921 Vavilov took over as head of the long-
standing Bureau of Applied Botany, founded in 1894 (pre-dating
by four years the United States' Office of Foreign Seed and Plant
Introduction).

Despite initially experiencing 'millions of troubles' in which
he was 'fighting against the cold at home, and for furniture, flats
and food', Vavilov managed to set up a new laboratory and
experimental station. As famine raged that year, Lenin allegedly
declared: 'The famine to prevent is the next one. And the time
to begin is now.' His support of science enabled Vavilov to turn
the Bureau of Applied Botany (now the N.I. Vavilov Institute
of Plant Industry, abbreviated from its Russian name to the VIR)
into a vast, plant-breeding empire. Under the umbrella of this

state-backed organisation, he was able to continue scouring the world on missions to collect seeds that might help him advance his theory.

In 1926 and 1927, Vavilov's travels took him to the Middle East, where, in the Fertile Crescent, agriculture first began. Despite being shot at and falling prey to malaria along the way, he first visited Lebanon and Syria and later Jordan, Palestine, Morocco, Algeria, Tunisia and Egypt. In his journals, he recalls coming across both cultivated and wild wheats:

> The very first excursions to Arabian villages revealed a field which displayed wheats of a peculiar composition. Here I collected for the first time the singular subspecies which I later named 'Khoranka'. This is a remarkably large-grained wheat with stiff straw and highly productive compact ears . . . And right here [in the Bekaa] – on the slopes and at the edges of the fields – I saw for the first time stands of wild wheat . . . But it was the drought resistance of the locally cultivated wheat, widely grown by the Arabian settlers, to which we gave our attention.

On their expeditions, Vavilov and his colleagues brought home in all between 148,000 and 175,000 samples of live seed and tubers to store for posterity. According to the Russian food historian G.A. Golubev, writing in 1979: 'Four-fifths of all the Soviet Union's cultivated areas are sown with varieties of different plants derived from the seeds available in the VIR's unique world collection.'

Today, scientists at the Millennium Seed Bank Partnership (MSBP) are very much aware of the enduring value of Vavilov's work. Through the Crop Wild Relatives Project they continue to seek out genetically diverse plants in order to preserve them, aided by partners worldwide, who each have detailed, expert knowledge of their own area. Eventually, the MSBP hopes to have specimens and examples of all the useful wild cousins of our domesticated plants, maps of where to find them, and information about how and when to collect them.

Through the work of the project, seeds of crop wild relatives from all over the world are classified, categorised, stored and made available to breeding programmes. It's a race against time to find and bank seeds before the wild plants succumb to threats such as climate change, urbanisation and deforestation. This urgency is illustrated all too clearly by the fate of *Solanum ruvu*, a wild relative of the aubergine, which was collected for the first time in Tanzania in 2000. By the time it had been identified as a new plant species, its native habitat had been destroyed and it is now considered extinct.

We now know that Vavilov was not quite correct in his view that centres of crop origin equated to centres of the highest diversity (in fact, the picture is a little more complicated, as high genetic diversity in a crop is influenced by geographic isolation and cultural diversity). Nevertheless, his work still informs studies undertaken by modern seed scientists, as the MSBP's Crop Wild Relatives Project Coordinator, Ruth Eastwood, explains:

The project has a master dataset that shows where a crop wild relative is present in the world today. We looked at herbarium specimens, used many geographical layers and applied a mathematical algorithm to model the distributions of those crop wild relatives. This generated precise maps of actual, known and assumed [modelled] distributions of wild crop relatives globally. The maps show us those areas that are richest for crop wild relatives. We've overlaid all those distributions on a map of those parts of the world that are the richest for crop wild relatives. When we look at that map now, it's amazing to realise that Vavilov's insights, all that time ago, with very limited data compared to what we have now and limited tools with which to analyse them, were actually pretty accurate.

For the man himself, his tragedy was the times he lived in. Sadly, he did not get long to enjoy the support given by Lenin to pursue his botanical mission. By the late 1920s the architect of the revolution was dead and Stalin had taken control of the Soviet Union, declaring 1929 to be the year of the 'Great Break with the Past'. The new leader short-sightedly believed that Vavilov should be concerned with the immediate work of reducing famine rather than wasting time on conserving genetic plant resources for the future. As a result, Stalin favoured Trofim Lysenko, who claimed he could get results more quickly than Vavilov in breeding plants that would help feed Russia's starving population.

Vavilov battled to fly the flag for Mendelian genetics as the basis for crop improvement but by the 1940s his Institute had been taken over by the ideas of Lysenko. And, as so many thinkers and intellectuals found to their cost, free thought was no defence in Stalin's Russia. In August 1940, while Vavilov was gathering wild grass specimens in the Carpathian Mountains, four men in a black sedan arrived to say he was urgently needed in Moscow. In fact, they had come to take him to prison in Saratov, the place in which his career in plant science had first begun.

The following year, while Vavilov was incarcerated and Germany was gaining ground across Europe in the Second World War, Stalin began shifting half a million treasures, including paintings, frescoes and gems, from the famous Hermitage gallery in Leningrad (renamed from Petrograd in 1924), to secret hiding places to protect them from Hitler's advancing armies. He felt no need to safeguard the 380,000 seeds, roots and fruits of the 2,500 species of food crops residing close by in Vavilov's seed bank.

But, by one of those miracles of the human spirit that run through the history of dark times, the seed bank survived the Siege of Leningrad. Its staff were not prepared to let Hitler plunder the immensely valuable resource that they and Vavilov had so painstakingly assembled. With Leningrad now cut off, and its people reduced to eating vermin, a group of scientists at the Bureau barricaded themselves inside the building and took shifts guarding the seeds in the pitch dark and subzero temperatures far below the frozen streets. Before them were containers of rice, peas, corn and wheat, but they refused to eat a single one. So it was that, while guarding one of the greatest collections of edible wild crop relatives ever to exist, nine of Vavilov's co-workers either starved to death or died of disease.

The collection's pioneering brainchild, meanwhile, succumbed to a slow death in prison in 1943. Vavilov, who had roamed five continents to gather wild crop seeds to stave off a recurrence of the famine he had experienced in childhood, died from the one thing he'd spent his life trying to prevent: starvation. Today, his story stands to remind us that science cannot succeed in bettering human life when politics fails.

15

BOTANICAL
MEDICINE

DIGITALIS *calycinis foliolis
ovatis, corollis obtusis, labio superiore
integro, Linn.*

G. D. Ehret, pinx.

Eighteenth-century illustration of *Digitalis*, the foxglove,
by Georg Dionysius Ehret

IN 1947, THE Nobel Prize for Chemistry was awarded to a British scientist and intellectual giant whose insights ranged across various aspects of organic chemistry. One of his greatest achievements was working out how to produce penicillin artificially in large quantities, saving millions of lives. But Sir Robert Robinson's award citation highlighted one area in particular: 'his investigations on plant products of biological importance, especially the alkaloids'. So, what are alkaloids and why are they of such high value?

Alkaloids are among a range of biochemical compounds produced by plants. Their role is not fully understood but they provide some protection for the plant against pathogens and herbivores. Unlike animals, plants cannot flee, so turn to chemistry to protect themselves, synthesising compounds – known as specialised or secondary metabolites – to counter threats. One property of many alkaloids is their bitter taste – as unappealing to numerous plant predators as it often is to humans. Of benefit to humans, however, is that these compounds can often be put to medicinal use.

Monique Simmonds, Deputy Keeper of Kew's Jodrell Laboratory, examines different aspects of the pharmaceutical potential of plant compounds. 'These compounds do not exist solely for our benefit,' she points out. 'Their purpose is usually protective – against insects, for example.' Some compounds, meanwhile, cause tiny pores found on plant leaves and stems to close. This is similar to processes in human cells that regulate our inflammatory response. These same compounds could have a potential as an anti-rheumatoid drug.

Morphine, now used as a powerful painkiller, was one of the earliest alkaloids to be discovered, in 1804, although its molecular structure was only finally untangled by Robinson in 1925. Other alkaloids include antimalarial treatments such as quinine and its modern derivatives, as well as compounds found in the Madagascar periwinkle (*Catharanthus roseus*), which have yielded treatments for childhood leukaemia and Hodgkin's disease.

Robinson's key breakthrough was in synthesising these powerful compounds (producing them from simpler materials by causing a chemical reaction), using the starting materials and conditions found in Nature. These new methods contrasted with previous ones, which relied on high temperatures and pressures to make the desired active chemical compounds. Robinson's initial success came with tropinone, used for treating certain heart conditions, bronchial problems and in eye surgery.

The use of medicinal plants goes back long before scientists had the tools to analyse which compounds could be associated with particular medicinal uses. Take the foxglove (*Digitalis purpurea*): its enchanting, often pink or purple bell-shaped flowers belie its poisonous nature, reflected by one of its nicknames, 'dead man's bells', yet people knew centuries ago of its healing power. English physician and botanist William Withering was inspired by traditional lore to try foxglove infusions as a treatment for dropsy (also known as oedema), a swelling of the legs due to fluid retention, often associated with congestive heart problems. He wrote that 'In the year 1775 my opinion was asked concerning a family receipt for the cure of the dropsy. I was told that it had long been kept secret by an old woman in Shropshire, who had sometimes made cures after the more regular practitioners had failed . . . This medicine was composed of 20 or more different herbs; but it was not very difficult for one conversant in these subjects to perceive that the active herb could be no other than the Foxglove.' He had an astonishing success rate among his patients of between 65 and 80 per cent. But it wasn't until the late 1800s that the active chemicals in foxgloves were isolated, with two leading compounds – digoxin and digitoxin – being singled out for their impact on regulating the heart.

There are few authentic historical records of willow bark as a herbal medicine, and it was chance that led to the publication of its medicinal properties. An English clergyman, Edward Stone, recorded, 'There is a bark of an English tree, which I have found by experience to be a powerful astringent, and very efficacious in curing agues [fevers] and intermitting disorders. About six years ago [in 1758], I accidentally tasted it, and was surprised at its extraordinary bitterness; which immediately raised in me a suspicion of its having the properties of the Peruvian bark [cinchona bark].' Stone gathered, dried and ground some willow bark, then experimented on the villagers near his home in rural Oxfordshire. He published his discovery of its effects on fevers in the leading scientific journal of the day, the *Philosophical Transactions of the Royal Society*. Interest in willow gradually increased, and a compound named salicin was found to be the active ingredient in 1828. Converted to salicylic acid in the laboratory, this was a highly effective pain-reliever, but was also linked to stomach upsets and ulcers. German scientists in 1899 altered salicylic acid to acetylsalicylic acid, which is safer for the stomach. This we more commonly know today as aspirin.

The opium poppy (*Papaver somniferum*) was also long prized for its medicinal properties as much as for the delicate beauty of its bright flowers and its distinctive round fruit casing, from the milky sap (or latex) of which opium is traditionally derived. Opium poppies appear in Greek and Roman texts as a medicine for dulling sorrow and pain; later, the Renaissance herbalist Paracelsus believed that opium could confer immortality. It also became the subject of two nineteenth-century wars, when the Chinese strongly objected to the British flooding their market with Indian opium. In 1803, its main active chemical became the first alkaloid to be isolated. Christened morphine, it went into commercial production in Germany in 1827.

This medicinal bounty naturally attracted the attentions of Kew. Between the late eighteenth century and the present day, medicinal plants from around the world came to Kew for propagation, study and dispersal to other gardens. Starting in the 1840s both Kew and the Royal Pharmaceutical Society collected the crude drugs too, as powdered bark, chopped root, dried leaves and myriad other preparations. Today Kew's Economic Botany Collection holds around 20,000 of these specimens. Its burnished wood cabinets bear witness to the efforts of intrepid plant hunters, pioneering pharmacologists and early drug manufacturers, in an era when at least three quarters of medicines were derived from plants. Recent additions to the Collection, including nearly 4,000 traditional Chinese medicines gathered over the last two decades, reflect the continuing movement of medicines and medical systems around the world.

Kew's cabinets served as training chests for pharmacists in the second half of the nineteenth century, priming them to recognise numerous plants thought to be effective for curing common Victorian maladies. Many were related to digestive complaints, in an era when gluttony seemed one of the lesser deadly sins. Purgatives included senna, Asiatic rhubarb (different to the British garden variety) and aloe – the latter as black latex whose effects bore no similarity to today's soothing gel. Oak galls were believed to be good for diarrhoea.

Papaveraceae.

Papaver somniferum L.

The opium poppy, long prized for its medicinal properties

More serious conditions also found their Victorian remedies in the Economic Botany Collection. Opium products such as laudanum were preferred painkillers for everyone from Queen Victoria, who used it in childbirth, to infants. The poison Shakespeare's Romeo famously took to kill himself, monkshood (*Aconitum napellus*), was widely used in solution to treat cases of fevers and 'sweats', as they were known. The treatment of fevers was of particular interest – not just in the expanding pink parts of the world map that marked Britain's Empire, but on the home front too, since fevers associated with what we now know to be malaria (then called 'agues') were prevalent every summer in marshy areas of London, Kent, Norfolk and Lincolnshire. Oliver Cromwell caught the disease in his youth and suffered from recurrent bouts of fever for the rest of his life. At the time these were attributed to the 'bad air' from which the word malaria comes.

It is one particular antimalarial that most colourfully links Kew with the history of medicinal plants. Over 1,000 specimens in its Economic Botany Collection relate to the development and use of cinchona. The bark of this tree had real medicinal bite, giving us quinine and various derivatives that target the *Plasmodium* parasites that cause malaria. The tree is reputedly named after the Spanish Countess of Chinchón who, legend has it, recovered from a fever in 1638 after having been treated with the bark, a native remedy known to Jesuit missionaries as 'quinquina' or 'bark of barks'.

Malaria was a scourge of the many European imperialists, the British among them, with ambitions in the tropics. Thousands died during explorations and campaigns in Africa and Asia, summed up neatly by one dark-humoured, nineteenth-century British sailors' refrain: 'Beware and take care of the Bight of Benin / There's one that comes out for forty goes in.' There was a pressing need to find a way to fight this disease, with cinchona and its antimalarial powers in the front line, but its collection posed two problems. One was that its native source lay in some of the most inaccessible parts of the Andes. The other was that there were around thirty or so species of cinchona, and no one was sure whether all or just some of them possessed the magic bark.

Dozens of expeditions set off with the aim of bringing back bark – and seeds – of the tree, with little success. Many collectors perished in the jungle. The eighteenth-century French explorer, Charles Marie de la Condamine (who also drew our attention to trees yielding rubber) managed to get the correct cinchona plants and seeds onto a boat bound for Europe, only for them to be swept overboard by a wave. As Mark Honigsbaum writes in his book on the subject, *The Fever Trail*, 'It was as if the tree was protected by some ancient Indian curse.'

Eventually trees and seeds successfully reached Europe. In 1820, the French chemists Pierre Joseph Pelletier and Joseph Caventou were the first to isolate quinine from cinchona bark in the laboratory, with Pelletier establishing a quinine extraction factory in Paris soon after. The British were not far behind in the race to exploit this crucial new medicine, with the pharmaceutical company Howards & Sons beginning production of quinine alkaloids in 1823. A scion of the family firm, John Eliot Howard became one of the most notable 'quinologists' of the Victorian era. His training as both a botanist and a chemist proved invaluable when evaluating sacks of cinchona bark at London's docks, an expertise he augmented by growing different species of cinchona in a greenhouse at his London home. The 30 or so species of cinchona look similar and hybridise easily, and each produces a different spectrum of medicinal alkaloids in its bark, but Howard was able to hone in on the most effective.

The dream, however, was to establish cinchona in places under British control, allowing quinine to be produced to a higher standard and at lower cost. Given the high mortality rate among the subjects of what was then British India, it is no surprise that the impetus came from the India Office. A British expedition was organised by Kew and travelled to South America in 1859–60. Seeds and plants were brought back to Kew by Richard Spruce and his fellow botanists, and sent on to India. Those plants that survived the rigours of the journey, and which proved to contain the quinine alkaloids, were widely planted in the hills of Darjeeling and southern India. In the 1860s extensive clinical trials were conducted by medical officers in Madras, Bombay and Calcutta. These showed that the combination of up to four quinine alkaloids found in Indian plantation bark was highly effective in treating malaria. An extensive distribution system was set up through Indian post offices to ensure that quinine could reach even the poorest people.

In contrast, the Dutch colony of Java established a thriving export industry based on cultivation of a variety of cinchona particularly rich in the main form of quinine alkaloid that was most favoured in European pharmacopeias. Seeds of this variety were later collected in Bolivia by Charles Ledger, working with his local Bolivian guide Manuel Incra Mamani – an all too rare case where we know the name of the local informants without whom none of the European plant collectors would have survived their journeys, let alone found their plants or understood their uses. Sadly, neither Ledger nor Mamani benefited much from their seed-collecting exploits; by the time the seeds arrived in London in 1865, the Indian plantations were well established and there was no interest from Kew. The seeds were sold for just 600 guilders (about £120) to the Dutch, and Mamani died a few years later after being arrested for smuggling seeds.

Cinchona trees in Madulsima, Ceylon (now Sri Lanka), 1882.
Quinine was extracted from the bark and used to treat malaria

The cultivation of cinchona in the Asian colonies of the Dutch and the British was timely. Because of the European demand for bark from its indigenous source, by the 1850s native stock in the Andes had been reduced by felling and tree stripping to the point of exhaustion.

By the 1930s, researchers had manipulated quinine to create chloroquine and primaquine, the first effective synthetic anti-malarial drugs. Malaria's increasing resistance to these treatments, however, drove the search for new compounds, culminating in the 1990s with the potent antimalarial arteminisin being isolated from sweet wormwood (*Artemisia annua*), native to temperate parts of Asia.

The discovery of arteminisin owed much to pointers that came from the plant's use in traditional Chinese medicine for treating fever, and historical and contemporary traditional knowledge continues to provide vital clues for those trying to identify medicinal plants. The importance of such leads becomes all too apparent when it is estimated that only about 20 per cent of the world's known plant species have been investigated for new compounds with potential medicinal properties.

Even so, around a quarter of all prescription drugs contain materials based on plant and fungal compounds, the latter having given us antibiotics, immunosuppressants, treatments for high cholesterol and anti-cancer drugs. Galantamine, used to treat mild to moderate Alzheimer's disease, is linked to ongoing research at Kew, and the compound tricin, isolated from rice, has been shown by collaborators in Leicester University to have the potential for treating breast cancer.

Kew's researchers have been at the forefront of furthering our knowledge about the profile of compounds in plants that could explain their traditional uses. 'Kew is seen as a trusted place,' says

Withania, Indian ginseng. Its biochemical properties are being researched for potential use in fighting dementia, arthritis, diabetes and cancer

Monique Simmonds. 'We get over 1,000 enquiries a year to help authenticate medicinal plants, of which about 35 per cent turn out to be not really fit for purpose as medicines, cosmetics and food. Sometimes it's the incorrect plant or the extract isn't right. We are most frequently asked to identify ginsengs. We check whether material in the trade is from the American or Asian species of ginseng, as the American one is covered by CITES (the Convention on International Trade in Endangered Species), which brings a conservation element to our work. Otherwise we're looking at whether toxins are present.'

Also at Kew, pharmacist Melanie Howes is working on medication for dementia derived from *Withania*. This pretty Indian native, with velvety leaves and dark orange berries wrapped in paper-thin sheaths, is commonly known as Ashwagandha or Indian ginseng (and sometimes winter cherry), with indicators as to its medical potential coming from its long use in Indian Ayurvedic healing as a tonic to combat fatigue, pain and stress.

Working with colleagues from Newcastle University, Howes investigated *Withania* root extract and found derivatives that tests suggested could be protective against two perceived causes of dementia. Other elements of the plant's biochemical arsenal are being investigated elsewhere for use in combating arthritis, diabetes and cancer.

Alongside ethnomedical pointers from traditional medicinal plant lore, there is a more modern hi-tech complement. DNA-based research has enabled botanists to understand better the relationships between plant species. This knowledge can help them to select plants that share similar biochemical properties, thus guiding their selection of plants for screening for potential medicinal use.

Kew's Herbarium has proven a lodestone for study, helping

researchers find plants yielding compounds with the potential to treat major killers. One example is the Moreton Bay chestnut (*Castanospermum australe*), a native Australian tree whose seeds yield a compound called castanospermine, which inhibits particular enzymes, including those involved in viral replication, and which has been used in the global battle against AIDS.

Kew is careful to strike a balance between the rights of local populations in the field and expert researchers back home in the laboratory. It is working with local communities in about 100 countries, in places that still rely heavily on plants as a source of medicine. 'It's a two-way benefit,' says Monique Simmonds. 'These are the most likely places where drugs of the future will come from, and if local plants lead to the development of new drugs, then the communities concerned should benefit. But it is not just about developing new drugs; it is also about respecting the rights of the communities and helping them conserve their natural assets.'

In certain parts of the world, such as sub-Saharan Africa, the majority of people – especially in poorer rural communities – rely more on medicinal plants than on the products of 'Big Pharma'. As Monique Simmonds admits, 'Some communities seem to place more trust in medicinal plants than in "drugs". It is important to understand why, as certain commercial products – especially vaccines – are highly valuable, and if people do not take them it could result in avoidable deaths.'

Preserving local knowledge is as vital as preserving the plants themselves. In some local communities in Ghana, for example, huge age gaps are appearing among those who know about their medicinal plants, with only 2 per cent of those aged between eighteen and twenty-seven claiming such knowledge, compared to a much higher figure for those aged between twenty-eight and fifty-seven. 'Fewer young people are aware of the uses of their plants, which is especially true in the urban areas,' says Monique Simmonds. 'In contrast, some villages still have elders with the expertise to select quality plant material.'

If we are to benefit from the study of traditional medicinal plants, there must be new and transparent strategies to ensure that such benefits are shared. Some must go to the local communities that have been the guardians of the plants' therapeutic use; some to the researchers who further our understanding of how the plants work; and some to the pharmaceutical companies that need to invest in the production of a safe drug from these leads.

16

SIGNALS OF GROWTH

ORIZA SATIVA L
Der gemeine Reiß.

Rice, the key plant in the discovery of the plant
hormone gibberellin

MAJOR BREAKTHROUGHS IN plant science are typically built on years of research and experimentation by many scientists. The Balzan Prize is one of the major honours for scientific fields not covered by the Nobels, and in 1982 the award – plus an accompanying $110,000 (£64,000) cheque – went to Kenneth Thimann. His discoveries marked the culmination of a journey that had previously embroiled Charles Darwin in a heated scientific spat, but this time, rather than evolution, the subject was plant hormones – biochemical substances produced by the plant that act on cells and tissues, ultimately influencing growth and behaviour

Born and educated in England, Thimann moved to America in 1930. His brilliance saw him make important strides in working out how plants make the pigments responsible for colour in flowers and fruits, the role of wavelengths of light in photosynthesis and the mechanisms of plant ageing. However, he is best known for his work in 1934 on the isolation and purification of the universal growth hormone auxin from plants.

Taking their name from the Greek verb *auxein* meaning 'to grow or increase', auxins are a group of hormones concerned with plant growth. They are made in the tips of the shoots and roots where they change the rate of elongation in plant cells, controlling their length. They are responsible for the curvature of plant shoots towards the light by causing elongation of cells on the side away from light (in which a greater concentration of auxin is found). They are also involved in the development of fruits. Auxins act in concert with, or in opposition to, other plant hormones to influence how plants behave. For example, the ratio of auxin to another hormone, called cytokinin, plays a role in the division of the plant's effort in terms of the development of roots versus that of buds.

Thimann's plant discovery was an auxin known as indole-3-acetic acid (IAA). His identification of the hormone's chemical structure led to the creation of synthetic versions of auxin, which became important tools in agriculture and horticulture. More controversially, his research was used by others to create Agent Orange, which was notoriously used to devastating effect against native populations in the Vietnam War to destroy crops and forests.

At Kew, auxins are used occasionally by horticulturalists to propagate rare plants where this may prove challenging by conventional means. Old plants can be particularly problematic, for example those being removed from the Temperate House, Kew's largest Victorian glasshouse, which is currently being restored. Normally, cuttings taken from these senescent, woody, slow-growing plants would die because the plants are tired, their bark is thick and they can't sprout roots fast enough to survive. Auxins solve the problem by speeding up the process. Greg Redwood, Head of Kew's Glasshouses, describes how it's done: 'We select the healthiest shoots, abrade the bark to expose the live tissue underneath, apply auxin rooting hormone to the wound, wrap in moss and tinfoil, then keep moist until the roots start to bud.' It's a procedure known as air layering.

As well as auxins spurring root growth, their importance in

botanical history lies in their crucial involvement in giving plants the ability to respond to external stimuli, allowing them to react to changing environmental conditions. Some have compared this to the nervous system of animals, a comparison that Thimann acknowledged, somewhat cautiously, in his book *Hormone Action in the Whole Life of Plants*:

> The concept that all the delicate adjustments of a complex organism like a flowering plant are made possible by the flow of diffusible chemicals is in some ways an elusive one. It has a curiously accidental quality and does not at first sight seem to be capable of sufficient precision. Perhaps it is for this reason that cranks are constantly coming up with claims that plants can appreciate music, be affected by prayer, or distinguish base motives in their watchers from charitable ones – powers that could only be exerted through the possession of a developed nervous system. While we can unhesitatingly dismiss such wishful thinking, it remains true that a nervous system gives a much more appealing impression of both delicacy and immediacy of control than does the secretion and flow of a group of chemical substances.

It is this connection between plant hormones and movement that links Thimann back to Darwin. The question of how plants move had intrigued people since the times of the ancient Greeks, with arguments raging between those who thought the movements were purely mechanical and those who believed they reflected some form of sensitivity or awareness in the plant to its surroundings.

It became an increasingly hot topic for plant scientists in the second half of the eighteenth century. Swiss naturalist Charles Bonnet conducted some of the earliest controlled experiments in plant movements. Charles Darwin's grandfather, Erasmus, was an early proponent of what was dubbed the Sensationalist position: that plants were sensitive organisms with a voluntary power of motion. He went so far as to argue that buds contained a brain that reacted to sensory stimuli, and also that plant behaviour relied at least in part on learned behaviour. This link to learning influenced his grandson's work on the subject in terms of how it might affect the evolution of plants.

Erasmus Darwin saw the behaviour of plants as a battle for resources to survive. Rather than relying merely on dry scientific discourse, however, he turned to poetry to express the concept. Here is a passage from his epic 1804 poem *Temple of Nature:*

> *Yes! Smiling Flora, drives her armed car,*
> *Through thick ranks of vegetable war;*
> *Herb, shrub, and tree with strong emotions rise*
> *For light and air, and battle in the skies:*
> *Whose roots diverging with opposing toil*
> *Contend below for moisture and soil.*

The early nineteenth century saw positions harden on both sides of the controlled versus mechanical movement debate, with Charles Darwin leaning firmly towards the former as he gathered evidence from a series of experiments conducted in the 1860s and 1870s. His key opponent was the German scientist Julius von Sachs, of photosynthesis fame, who was adamant that plants did not possess any cells with the specific ability to sense their surroundings, and certainly none allowing an active adjustment to their environment.

Almost immediately after publishing *On the Origin of Species*, Darwin became fascinated by the movements of the bog-loving, carnivorous sundew *Drosera rotundifolia.* In a letter of November

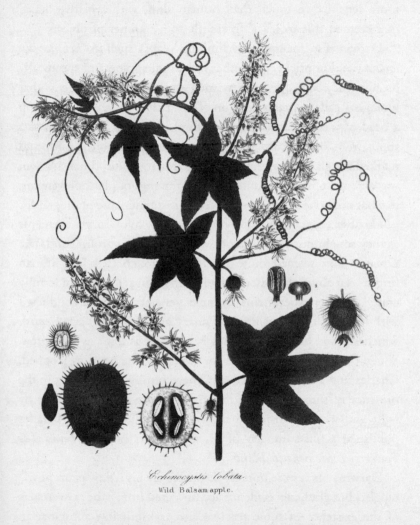

Echinocystis lobata.
Wild Balsam apple.

Wild balsam apple (*Echinocystis lobata*) used by Darwin in his
experiments on the movement of plants

1860 to the lawyer and geologist Charles Lyell, he exclaims that he was 'frightened and astounded' by it, shocked to find a plant more sensitive to touch than human skin, with sensitive 'hairs' that seemed able to react differently to a number of objects.

Darwin also focused on climbing plants such as *Echinocystis lobata* (wild or prickly cucumber or balsam apple), and specifically on how they controlled the twisting and twining movements that biologists called circumnutation. To test this, he visually lined up a bead of wax on a glass needle affixed to a plant organ such as a shoot, root or leaf, along with a stationary dot on a card, and marked the glass. By repeatedly doing this at various times, Darwin was able to connect the dots to create tracings of plant movement, in what might be considered a precursor to time-lapse photography.

He observed tendrils displaying probing, exploratory movements as they sought out something to wrap themselves around and, like *Drosera*, they seemed more sensitive to touch than the human finger – an ability he described admiringly in 1863 as 'wonderfully crafty'. Further experiments – simple, yet elegant – were conducted with his son Francis, using the Canary grass (*Phalaris canariensis*), which showed how its seedlings bent towards light as they grew. When they covered the tips of the seedlings, the bending stopped. Charles and Francis concluded: 'These results seem to imply the presence of some matter in the upper part which is acted on by light and which transmits its effects to the lower part.' Charles published a full summary of his theories in his 1880 book *The Power of Movement in Plants*.

Darwin's ideas were initially dismissed by his fellow plant physiologists but gradually evidence accumulated from other researchers of the existence of some reactive and transmissible substance in plant tips. Although an auxin compound had been detected in the by-products of fermentation by German biochemist Ernst

Sakowlski in 1885, the first auxin to be isolated and purified was auxentriolic acid (also known as Auxin A), found in human urine by Fritz Kogl and Arie Jan Haagen-Smit in 1931. Later Kogl isolated other compounds from urine that were similar in structure and function to Auxin A, one of which was indole-3 acetic acid (IAA) – the compound Thimann first isolated in plants soon after.

While auxins are a particular boon for horticulturalists wanting their cuttings to root quickly, in terms of agriculture it is another plant hormone that has seized the limelight. Its discovery owes much to a rice disease that Japanese farmers called *bakanae*, or foolish seedling. The name came about because the rice kept growing taller and taller until it simply fell over, as useless as a drunk in the gutter.

In 1898, Japanse researcher Shotaro Hori showed that the problem was caused by a fungus, and in 1935, Teijiro Yabuta was able to isolate a specific molecule from the fungus that caused the unrestrained growth, which he christened gibberellin. But it wasn't until after the Second World War that news of the discovery spread through the scientific community. Then the race was on to work out how gibberellin acted on plants. This research would lead to dwarf varieties of key crops that transformed global production fifty years ago in what was dubbed the Green Revolution.

Nick Harberd, Sibthorpian Professor of Plant Science at St John's College, Oxford, takes up the story of one of the Green Revolution's biggest triumphs. 'During the 1950s–60s Norman Borlaug bred a high-yielding dwarf wheat – others were also doing something similar with dwarf rice – which was very productive because it directed resources into yield, not stem growth. If yields go up, people get fed.' Borlaug's dwarf wheat was credited with saving perhaps a billion people from starvation in Mexico, Pakistan and India – an achievement that earned him the 1970 Nobel Peace Prize.

Pomme Princesse

à l'Imprimerie de Langlois

Plant hormones play an important role in the ripening of fruits,
such as the apple

Plant invader: *Lantana camara* (*left*), is native to South America but was introduced first to Europe, then to Calcutta's botanical garden (in 1807). It spread with such great vigour that 100 years later it was threatening teak plantations. Today 650 varieties are causing mayhem across 60 countries

Islands are vulnerable to invasives. The parsley fern, *Anogramma ascensionis* (*right*), unique to Ascension Island, was declared extinct in 2003, probably due to the introduction of maidenhair ferns which aggressively colonised the parsley fern's habitat. It was spotted again on the slopes of Green Mountain (*below*) and a conservation project involving Kew is now under way to ensure its survival

The European beech (*Fagus sylvatica*) spreads its tree canopy to draw energy direct from the sun. The key to this is a biomolecule called chlorophyll contained in the leaves, which also gives them their green colour

The treescape as depicted in *The Hay Wain* by John Constable is unrecognisable to those born after 1970, Europe's elm population having been destroyed by Dutch elm disease

A diseased elm showing classic wilt and withering of leaves on specific branches of the tree

Wild cinchona bark from South America, analysed by John Eliot Howard, the notable 'quinologist', with results on its label. The bark was the source of quinine used to treat malaria

From the 1840s both Kew and the Royal Pharmaceutical Society of Great Britain collected crude drugs as powdered bark, chopped root, dried leaves and other preparations. This cabinet was used to train pharmacy students

Gathering the opium from punctured seed heads in India. The opium poppy has a long history of medicinal use

Gathering Opium from the Capsules in the "Sitooah" or scraper after incision

Medicinal plants on sale today in Brazil (*left*) and in Anguo, China (*below*)

Trifolium Acetosum flo: albo.   Rosa Damascena flore
pleno.   Trifolium Acetosum flore flavo.

Botanical illustrations centuries apart.
Hand-coloured engraving depicting rose with white and yellow clover
from Basilius Besler's *Hortus Eystettensis*, first published in 1613

Gustavia longifolia by
contemporary artist
Lucy T. Smith, held in
the extensive library and
art collections at Kew

Devastation caused by the 1987 hurricane at Kew's country estate, Wakehurst Place, West Sussex (*above*). The hurricane had surprising benefits, transforming understanding and practice of tree planting and arboreal care

Harberd's team has been at the forefront of working out what he describes as 'the molecular identity of dwarfism', caused by genes that repress the production of gibberellin. It also affects seed and fruit size. Harberd's research is shedding light on how the manipulation of the relevant genes that control how the hormone acts may help develop crops suitable for some of the harsher environments – arid or saline, for example – being created by global climate change.

Like auxins, gibberellins are a group of hormones rather than a single compound. So far 136 gibberellins have been identified. And because their effect varies, depending on the type of gibberellin and the species of plant, they present growers with an impressive armoury of benefits. As well as their role in producing dwarf varieties, gibberellins are used to encourage fruit setting in apples and pears, counteracting the tendency of these trees to take a 'year off' after a heavy-cropping year. Gibberellic acid sprays, meanwhile, fatten grapes to the size demanded by the modern consumer.

Synthetic auxins are at the forefront of modern agricultural practice at places such as the National Fruit Collection at Brogdale. One auxin, called NAA, is used to sustain the yield of perfectly ripe fruit; sprayed on as the fruit matures, it keeps the crop on the tree until it is fully mature and ready for harvesting.

Another feature of auxins is that they trigger plants to naturally release the gaseous hormone ethylene, which is strongly linked to fruit ripening. Many plants emit ethylene naturally – bananas are particularly renowned for it – and it has been claimed historically that the ancient Egyptians used this fact to stimulate fig-ripening. Similarly, there are tales of the ancient Chinese burning incense in closed rooms to speed the ripening of pears. Today, hormonal ethylene induction is used to accelerate the maturing of apples and tomatoes, or to synchronise fruit setting in pineapples.

Other categories of plant hormones have been discovered and analysed for the ways in which they might benefit agriculture and horticulture. Cytokinins, for example, are used for regulating growth and tackling leaf ageing. Ageing has been found to be delayed in plants with an excess of cytokinin, so by manipulating levels of the hormone it should be possible to extend the period in which the leaves continue to photosynthesise and therefore improve productivity. Tobacco, grown for its all-important leaves, is providing the prime test-bed for this.

Brassinosteroids, meanwhile, are hormones that show promise of boosting yields for crops such as potato, rice, barley and wheat. Intriguingly, they appear to work particularly well in difficult conditions. When they were applied to crops under optimal conditions, they had little effect, while crops grown under conditions of stress, for example rice seeds treated with brassinosteroids and grown in sub-optimal salt conditions, showed better than expected yields compared with untreated plants. Clearly there is much to be learned from foolish seedlings.

17

UNLOCKING
BIODIVERSITY

Flora Graeca, produced between 1806 and 1840, one of the
all-time botanical masterworks

I N THE COOL of the library on the first floor of Kew's Herbarium a series of windows set into a wall allow the visitor to gaze into a vast store room and look at its rich collection of rare books, now held in strictly climate-controlled conditions. Here are kept the library's most precious items, many in leather-bound volumes, some dating from as far back as the late fifteenth century. One example is the *Flora Graeca*, by Oxford botanist John Sibthorp and Ferdinand Bauer, the renowned Austrian botanical illustrator, produced between 1806 and 1840, which eventually ran to ten separate volumes. In 1786–7, the two men had made a research voyage to the eastern Mediterranean, but it took the next fifty years to publish their results. Such were the technical and financial difficulties that only sixty-five sets were published. However, their hard work was justified, for the book would come to be regarded as one of the all-time botanical masterworks, fetching a fortune on the open market. Its pages are a delight to behold, with graceful engravings capturing each species that they discovered.

Although these Floras are fascinating to examine and – with their beautiful hand-coloured plates – aesthetically very pleasing, their real significance lies not in their monetary or historical value, but in the record they make of biodiversity. Such early Floras mark the beginning of our efforts to describe all the species growing in a particular region or locality, marking a turning point in our attitude towards the earth's riches. They also give us a baseline from which to measure the appearance or disappearance of other recorded species at that particular spot. And whilst these volumes might have originally been produced for wealthy clients, keen to impress their peers by exhibiting knowledge gathered from across the globe, in the twenty-first century they remind us just how useful a tool for science the recording of an area's flora can be.

Producing Floras remains a fundamental part of Kew's work to this day. By a Flora, we mean a record documenting all the wild plant species known to grow in a geographical area (sometimes also including introduced species and invasives). The intention of a Flora is to allow readers to identify these species. Although it is called a 'Flora', such a record also normally includes non-flowering species such as conifers, mosses and ferns.

In the past, Floras were bound volumes: either 'Field floras', smaller books for carrying into the field for identification purposes, or larger and more detailed Floras for perusal on return home. For reasons of economy and usefulness, many modern Floras are now appearing online or as e-books, which makes them available to users without access to botanical libraries, as well as permitting them to be used on small hand-held devices, making them portable for use in the field.

Yet the process of compiling a Flora, no matter what form it eventually takes, remains the same as that followed by Sibthorp and Bauer in the final years of the eighteenth century. It begins when the botanist visits the area concerned, collecting specimens and keeping meticulous records of their finds. In particular, they must develop a system for recording lifelike colours, which are highly likely to fade long before finished images can be prepared.

A plant press used as a makeshift seat, on expedition in
Northern Transvaal in 1930

They must also find a way of evoking the growth of the plant,
which is not always obvious from a pressed specimen. The specimens collected must be preserved in such a way as to allow the
fine anatomy of the plant to be conveyed home for greater study.
Lastly, the botanist must record the locations and habitat in which
the plant was found and the date on which it was collected.

Once the botanist has returned home with his or her collections, another stage of the work begins. The plant must be correctly
named, with its scientific (Latin) name. A Flora will also list those
botanical names that are synonyms, other botanical names that
have been used to describe it. This might occur, for example, if
the plant was formerly considered to be a separate species but is
now being incorporated under the umbrella of another. Some
notes will also be included, explaining, for example, the range of

flower colour, or the flavour of its fruits, as well as information on the kinds of habitats favoured by the plant.

Iain Darbyshire, Head of the Africa Drylands team at Kew, explains. 'You're creating order out of chaos. You start off with a group of dried specimens in the Herbarium that often have either been given incorrect names, or none at all. There are hundreds of specimens to work through, and it's such a satisfying procedure to do this, ending up with correct names for each of the species, together with our knowledge of how to identify them. This information is so useful for those in the field in every discipline, whether land managers, ecologists, botanists or research scientists.'

The species treated in a Flora will be based on as many collections as possible, not only the recent specimens from collecting expeditions but also those held in herbaria, potentially dating back as far as the seventeenth century. Most Floras will cite a selection of the specimens examined so that the species record can easily be verified by future researchers. In addition to detailed descriptions of each species, a Flora will contain identification keys as well as notes on the habitat and distribution of each species and sometimes its conservation status.

The *Flora of Tropical East Africa* is one of the biggest flora survey projects ever to have been undertaken at Kew. It began in 1948 with the aim of cataloguing all identified wild plant species known to grow in the three countries of Uganda, Kenya and Tanzania. At the beginning, it was expected to cover only about 7,000 species. Although originally estimated to take fifteen years to complete, in actual fact this epic project took sixty, and the eventual Flora was finished only in September 2012, its final tally exceeding 12,100 species. When published in book form, it took up 263 volumes, occupying about a metre and a half of shelf space. One hundred and thirty-five botanists worked on the project, in twenty-one

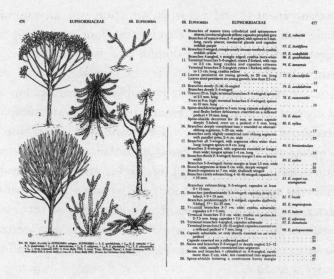

Pages from the *Flora of Tropical East Africa*, one of the biggest
flora survey projects ever, covering 12,100 species

countries, and during its compilation they described some 1,500
species that were completely unknown to science. In the last four
years of the project alone, 114 new species were added.

Arguably the most biodiverse area in Tropical Africa, and one
of the richest floras in the world, this region contains an enormous
variety of habitats, ranging from the grassland savannah of the
Serengeti to the Ugandan rainforest, and a moorland on the shoulder
of Kilimanjaro. It is also home to a very high number of 'endemic'
species – plants that occur in a single region or area. These endemics
are a clear conservation priority, as their loss in this part of the
world would mean their global extinction. Yet in East Africa, when
the project began in 1948, there was no existing list of the plants
growing there at all.

As a consequence, a Flora can be a powerful tool for attracting attention, research and conservation efforts to an area. Henk Beentje, former head of the East Africa Flora project, highlights a number of rare plants, including one from Tanzania that is known solely from a single hillside, commenting, 'A Flora enables you to name the species, and it enables communication about wild species. If there is no Flora, you can't communicate with others about it, and scientific work doesn't even get off base.' Iain Darbyshire adds: 'Until we know a number of things – what the total species diversity in a region is; where the most diverse areas within that region can be found; and what are the rarest, most threatened species, we can't do effective conservation nor prioritise it properly. We also need to work out which are the threatening, invasive species, documenting where they first occurred and where they are spreading.'

One important use of Floras in the conservation setting is in negotiations with big companies such as construction and mining enterprises. As Henk Beentje says, 'There is a lot of development going on in East Africa, which is one reason we need to document all these species.' Quentin Luke, a freelance botanist associated with the National Museums of Kenya, and an Honorary Kew Associate based in Nairobi, explains: 'What I do is work on environmental impact assessments for mines, roads and all sorts of development. In areas where Floras haven't been done, you have to collect plant samples completely blind, and when you get back to base you find you've missed the rare stuff. In the field, you can sort that out with a Flora. If you can show that there are species of conservation significance within the area of impact, the companies concerned have to do something about it.'

Floras can also provide surprises. The African violet is an iconic species of the region, enormously popular as a houseplant in the UK and grown commercially by the horticulture industry in a trade that amounts to some US $75 million (£44 million) a year, mainly in hybrids. *Saintpaulia*, as it is known botanically, is one of the most economically significant traded plants in the world. Iain Darbyshire, who has been working on the plants for the Flora, describes the contrasting situation for the species in the wild: 'There are less than ten species of *Saintpaulia* in the world, and all are threatened with extinction. They originate from Kenya and Tanzania, and they are extremely rare, restricted to very small patches of low-altitude forest. They've become a real flagship group for conservation in the region, because they are associated with some of the most species-rich forests in Africa.'

When asked: 'Do you ever really finish a Flora?' Henk Beentje's answer is very clear. 'No. You need to keep on updating. As soon as you publish a Flora, people will be able to use what you have written, which usually results in new records and sometimes even in new species being discovered. We still are finding new species in East Africa.'

Some information is traditionally left out of Floras. Local names for plants are frequently excluded, even though for ethnobotanists, for example, who collect background information on local medical plant practices, this might be the most useful aspect. One of the advantages of the new Floras on the internet is that intelligence of this kind can be more often included via hyperlinks.

Today Kew is a passionate advocate for the creation of e-Floras. The intention is to utilise Kew's massive expertise in the subject and apply it, always with the goal of widening access to botanical knowledge. The *Flora Zambesiaca*, for example, which covers the entire basin of the Zambezi river (including Zambia, Malawi, Mozambique, Botswana and Zimbabwe), is now digitised and available online. The skills developed in creating and holding these digital versions of Floras have been shared with botanic gardens

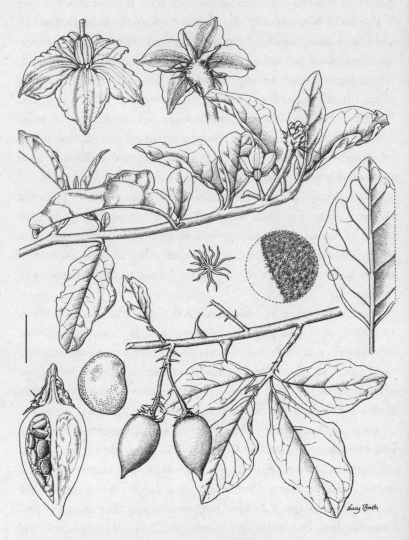

The work of the botanical artist, *Solanum phoxocarpum*, from Africa, by Lucy T. Smith

undertaking similarly ambitious tasks, such as the digitisation of the *Flora Malesiana* (which covers much of South-East Asia from Indonesia to Papua New Guinea) at Leiden Botanic Garden, Holland's most distinguished authority in the field. Kew, in tandem with other world-class institutions, has now committed itself to an ambitious goal: having the whole world's flora online with universal access by the year 2020.

One thing that will not change, however, is the way in which Floras are illustrated. Even as they make their way onto the internet and hand-held devices for use in remote parts of the planet, photographs are not replacing drawings; botanical artists are still required to produce the images that the Floras contain.

Lucy Smith, one of Kew's botanical artists, explains her working process, using a specimen of a new grass species she has been working on with the aid of a microscope: 'I work from the macro, larger scale right down to the micro scale. I begin by drawing what we call the "habit" of the plant. If that's a tree or a shrub, that might be a few leaves on a branch with some flowers or fruits; but if it's a piece of grass, I will include the whole plant, to illustrate the roots, the rhizome, the stem, the leaves and the way they are attached, and eventually the flowers too.

'So,' she continues, 'I show the habit of the plant, and then a close-up of where the flowers emerge from it. There is a close-up of how the leaves wrap around the sheath of the grass. Then I go into the flowering details, because they're really important in identifying the differences between species. Next I show the florets, and the bracts that enclose them. And some of these florets are really tiny; this one I've illustrated here is probably about 5 millimetres in length.' She is clear on the challenges facing a botanical artist: 'The artist's drawing skills definitely come into play here at Kew, because a lot of the specimens we're presented with have been pressed in a plant press out in the field somewhere, and brought back not in the best state; so their leaves will be folded and crumpled, sometimes broken. You really have to use your drawing skills to bring that plant back to life.'

It is partly because of this careful editing and interpretation that the artist remains necessary in preparing a visual depiction of any species. 'You get rid of extraneous details of a plant, but focus on and highlight those that are important and really need to be seen. You can edit too, while making sure that the key characteristics are there and that they're sharp. You're clarifying. With a photograph, you just see one aspect of the plant at a single point in its life. With an illustration, all the different parts of the plant are put into one plate, one image, so it's all there, it's all to scale and it's all in one place.'

As Kew moves through the twenty-first century, this beautiful, old-fashioned skill, so in evidence in its library collections, will remain an essential element of even its most modern Flora projects. When the world Flora is eventually finished, botanical artists' illustrations will still form a central part of its riches.

18

AN ILL WIND

A post-storm arrival of a new tree at Kew

D URING THE EARLY hours of 16 October 1987, hurricane-force winds ripped through southern England, with recorded gusts of 110mph felling 15 million trees across the country in a few hours. This, however, is the story of how one Kew oak tree that didn't fall helped transform the understanding and practice of tree planting and arboreal care.

The Turner oak (*Quercus* × *turneri)* is a cross between *Quercus robur* (the English oak) and *Quercus ilex* (the holm or holly oak). It takes its name from the Kew nurseryman who bred it in 1783. He also helped Kew founder Princess Augusta plant the tree in its present location in 1798, near the lake created by Sir William Hooker in 1861, which was later augmented with waterside plantings by his illustrious son Joseph.

The Turner oak's widespread branches have made it a popular sheltering spot for visitors over two centuries. But as hurricane gusts and downpours raged in the darkness of the Great Storm, there was no one present to witness the moment the old oak was lifted bodily from its long earthy embrace, teetered on the verge of falling, then dropped vertically back into place.

Dawn revealed over 700 of Kew's trees sprawled on their sides, their root systems exposed to the cool air in the calm after the storm. In the face of this arboreal carnage, the Turner oak was very much a low priority, especially given the tree's increasingly moribund state before the storm. Standing on its mulched bed today, Tony Kirkham, Head of Kew's Arboretum, takes up the story: 'Before the Hurricane, it was going into decline, with a very thin canopy, lots of epicormic growth [suckers along its main trunk and scaffolds] and clear signs of stress. It was probably on its way out. So we said we'd leave it to the end of the clearance. We had 700 other trees to deal with, which took three years. Then we came back to the Turner oak – and it was a picture of health.'

Piecing clues together, the Kew team first grasped that 200 years of people standing beneath the Turner oak's branches had caused a problem that no one had realised existed. 'It was suffering badly from compaction – and this tree was de-compacted overnight,' explains Kirkham. 'Very aggressively, yes, but nevertheless the root-ball was shaken; the ground was opened up; the movement of both air and water was boosted. This tree was revitalised, putting on a third of its total growth since the storm.'

Being suddenly presented with 700 upended trees provided a unique opportunity to examine the root systems of myriad species in what became the Kew root survey. One key realisation was how shallow tree roots are – contrary to the old arborists' saying of 'What you see above ground is what you get below ground'. In fact, latest opinion suggests that temperate tree roots generally go down a metre or less.

The upended root plates revealed that most of the trees at Kew were suffering from compaction. The solution that Tony Kirkham came up with involved the novel use of a tool called the Terravent, previously employed for aerating sports pitches. 'Today we use another tool called the AirSpade, which actually mimics the hurricane of 1987 in a less aggressive manner, by blowing compressed air into

Seven hundred upended trees provided a unique opportunity
to study root systems

the ground,' he explains. 'It shatters the soil structure without cutting
through roots, opening up compacted earth. Most trees respond to
it – and it's now used by arborists all over the world.'

The root survey also prompted Kew's tree planters to make
their holes square. 'Previously, everyone planted trees in round
holes but the trees weren't establishing strong roots, so we had to
stake them,' explains Kirkham. 'However, we know from the nursery
that when you put a tree in a round pot or hole, you get spiralling
roots – they don't extend outwards. So we started looking at square
holes, because the weakest part of a square hole, as far as the roots
are concerned, is the corner and the more corners there are, the
more chance you have of roots breaking through there. If you
have four corners, you have potentially four breakthrough points.'

Having so many trees reveal their roots at one time led to a better view of how trees actually stay upright, despite shallow roots. 'Trees *need* wind,' argues Kirkham. 'We're all paranoid about wind but trees have to bend to get used to standing upright. When we planted trees before, we used to overstake them so that they couldn't move – but then they couldn't develop a strong root system. It's all about balance and friction. This year we planted 200 trees and not one of them is staked.'

Vitally, the 1987 hurricane provided Kew with a beneficial natural clear-out. This once-in-a-generation chance to rethink the Gardens' arboreal canvas prompted a long-overdue audit, which suddenly pointed to gaps in the wooded plant collection, at Kew as well as in the temperate woodland at Wakehurst Place in West Sussex, Kew's 465-acre country garden estate, at that time overseen by Mark Flanagan. Different approaches have guided replanting at the two locations.

At Wakehurst, the ongoing guiding principle has been phyto-geography – basically, a planting system based on the geographical origin and distribution of species. This draws on work by the likes of Alfred Russel Wallace who, in addition to co-discovering the principle of natural selection with Darwin, worked on geograph-ical patterns in species diversity. 'It's like creating a global map,' explains Kirkham, conjuring up a beguiling image of a sylvan stroll across the planet. 'At Wakehurst you can go to America, then walk down to Mexico, then across to Taiwan – you can go round the world, looking at all those country's trees.'

Geographic planting at Wakehurst Place was not in itself a new approach. It had been followed before the 1987 hurricane, in areas of the estate such as the Southern Hemisphere Garden, established by Gerald Loder between 1902 and 1936, and also in the continental gardens representing America, Asia and Europe, planted between 1965 and 1987.

Highlights from these plantings include the national collection of Asian-origin birches as well as one of Southern beeches – the latter featuring two species, *Nothofagus glauca* and *N. alessandrii*, which are threatened with extinction in the wild. Britain's rarest trees are also here, including the Plymouth pear (*Pyrus cordata*) and scarce microspecies of *Sorbus*, covering rowans, service trees and whitebeams.

Post-1987, Andrew Jackson, Head of Wakehurst Place, says that the gardens there have developed a 'much more sophisticated planting scheme that brings to life stories about plate tectonics, plants that survived ice-ages, co-evolution, etc.'. This was inspired by a book entitled *Floristic Regions of the World* by the Armenian botanist Armen Takhtajan, who visited Wakehurst to see the launch of the new planting scheme in 1991.

Like Kirkham at Kew, Jackson believes that Wakehurst has benefited from the carnage of the Great Storm, not least in the ongoing flood of intriguing new arrivals. 'It probably has the single greatest collection of post-storm planting of trees from around the temperate world,' he says. 'New introductions from the wild have come from China, Japan, Pakistan, Australia, New Zealand, Argentina, Chile, Mexico, the USA, Canada, Russia, North Africa and Turkey. Most have been made by Kew's horticultural staff.'

In contrast to Wakehurst's method of planting according to geographical origin, Kew's post-hurricane reorganisation reflects the historic nineteenth-century classifications of Joseph Hooker. This was grandly encapsulated in *Genera Plantarum*, co-written with George Bentham, describing 7,569 genera and around 100,000 species of seed-bearing plants – the vast majority of them having been deposited in Kew's Herbarium. The nineteenth-century approach is complemented by insights from the Angiosperm Phylogeny Group's new classification, APG III, drawn from modern

The root survey prompted Kew's tree planters to
make their holes square

research using DNA analysis to help define the evolutionary relationships between plants (see Chapter 21), although, as Kirkham
points out, for trees, APG III is very close to Hooker's system.
'We maintain that in the Arboretum for heritage and scientific
reasons.'

Another benefit of post-hurricane arboreal reinvention at both
Wakehurst and Kew has been plant hunting. 'We started a new
era of plant exploration, targeting places where we were weak –
Taiwan, South Korea, the Russian Far East, China,' says Kirkham.
'And we have places we want to go back to again, like Japan and
the Caucasus.'

It isn't just far-flung destinations that Kew's latest generation
of plant hunters are eyeing up though. There are British trees
on Kirkham's shopping list too, such as *Sorbus lancastriensis* (the

Lancaster whitebeam). 'Whilst I haven't got a good specimen here, there are probably around 2,000 growing near Arnside and Carnforth in Cumbria. So yes, we do go to China – but there are also excellent trees on our own doorstep. You learn so much by going into native forest,' enthuses Kirkham. 'You find out what trees want and how different ones grow. You look at plant associations, how big the trees get, the aspect, whether or not they grow near a river. It really focuses the mind.'

One of the more remarkable examples of the post-hurricane replanting has brought to Kew a tree previously thought to have become extinct 2 million years ago. Formerly known only through fossil records, the so-called Wollemi pine (which is part of the Araucariaceae family of ancient conifers that includes the monkey puzzle tree) was rediscovered in 1994, when around 100 of the Australian species *Wollemia nobilis* were found in a temperate rainforest gorge inside the Wollemi National Park about 100 miles from Sydney, Australia.

In 1997, a decade after the Great Storm, Sydney's Royal Botanic Gardens presented Kew with two seedlings and thirty seeds of the Wollemi pine. The seeds were stored in the Millennium Seed Bank at Wakehurst, while the seedlings were grown on. In 2005, Sir David Attenborough planted one of the young saplings at Kew – the first to be planted outdoors outside Australia – while the other was given a place in the Southern Hemisphere Garden at Wakehurst.

Both are now healthy young trees, providing Kew's scientists with a chance to study a living arboreal fossil. The Wollemi pine's scarcity in the wild means little is still known about it, apart from a few basics about the fertility of its male and female cones, its slow-growing status, plus its extreme longevity – some of the Australian trees are estimated to be between 500 and 1,000 years old. Visitors to Kew wishing to plant for the distant future can do some studying themselves by buying specimens of the pine at the Gardens' Victoria Gate shop.

While growing a Wollemi pine is definitely a long-term project for any tree-lover, the Great Storm provided a counter-balancing lesson about time, as Kirkham revealed on a walk through the Arboretum. 'Ninety per cent of the tree planting here has been done since 1987,' he says, gesturing to a well-established arboreal vista. 'This perhaps disproves the old arborists' saying that "You're always planting for the next generation."'

Clearly, the 1987 hurricane has been good for Kew, both in terms of knowledge and of a fresh, bolder mindset. Take what has happened to the Gardens' famous Broad Walk, laid out in 1845–6 by landscape architect William Andrews Nesfield – also known for designing spectacular water features such as the 120-jet Witley Court Fountain in Worcestershire and the Prince of Wales fountain at Kew's northern outpost, the Yorkshire Arboretum at Castle Howard. The Broad Walk soon became one of Kew's most iconic vistas. Yet for much of its existence it also suffered an arboreal jinx. Nesfield's original planting of deodara cedars (*Cedrus deodara*) was all but lost through London's increasing pollution in combination with the dry soil, while the Atlantic cedars (*Cedrus atlantica*) planted in their stead at the turn of the twentieth century fared equally badly. These were replaced by North American tulip trees (*Liriodendron tulipifera*), with a similar lack of success.

It was only in 2000, armed with knowledge gained in the aftermath of the hurricane, that Kew removed all but two of the tulip trees and replanted sixteen semi-mature Atlantic cedars – but ones specifically brought from Morocco's Atlas Mountains to tolerate Kew's particular conditions. The trees flourish today as a fine acknowledgement of Nesfield's original vision. As Kirkham says, 'We did this only because the 1987 hurricane gave us the impetus to change.' One old saying was right: 'It is an ill wind that blows nobody any good.'

19

CAPSULES OF LIFE

Seeds of the English plaintain, *Plantago lanceolata*

S EEDS ARE CAPSULES of life waiting to begin. Their vast array of sizes, shapes and colours reflect adaptations made by plants over millions of years to maximise their chances of survival within particular environments. Only if specific requirements are met – whether for temperature, humidity, the presence of fire or mycorrhizal fungi – will a plant's seeds germinate and prosper. Wolfgang Stuppy, Seed Morphologist at the Millennium Seed Bank Partnership (MSBP), is enthusiastic about his subject. 'Seeds can tell you an awful lot about a plant's lifestyle and evolution through the millennia. If a seed does not achieve what it is supposed to, that species becomes extinct. So every plant you see around today must somehow work in its natural habitat. And that is often surprising when you look at all the crazy variety in seeds that you encounter in the wild.'

The MSBP is one of around 1,750 seed banks that exist in the world today. As we have seen in Chapter 14, the world's first seed banks were established in Russia and the USA at the beginning of the twentieth century. Seed collectors such as Nikolai Vavilov realised that selective breeding by farmers down the centuries had gradually reduced the genetic diversity contained within crop seeds, and sought to save their genetically rich, wild crop 'relatives'. By the 1980s, concern was turning towards the fate of wild plants and their ecosystems, which were threatened by logging, urbanisation and human-induced climate change. The Convention on Biological Diversity – launched in 1992 at the United Nations Conference on Environment and Development (the Rio Earth Summit) – suggested in Article 9 that contracting parties should complement *in situ* conservation of biodiversity, conducted within the natural environment, with *ex situ* (externally undertaken) methods. The banking of seeds is one *ex situ* method used for conserving genetic material from plants.

Modern seed banks range from small facilities kept by individual botanic gardens to major international banking programmes. The Svalbard Global Seed Vault, built deep inside a mountain in the Arctic, acts as a back-up by storing duplicate samples of crop seeds held by other such banks around the globe. Meanwhile, the MSBP stores seeds from wild species, both edible and non-edible. By 2020 it aims to bank seeds from 25 per cent of the world's plants, prioritising those that are endemic (unique to a particular location), economically valuable and endangered.

'Plants sit at the base of the food chain, providing food all the way up to us at the top,' explains Paul Smith, Head of the MSBP. 'They contribute to soil formation and nutrient cycling, and they provide us with shelter, medicines and fuel. Despite this, the Millennium Ecosystem Assessment [an appraisal of the condition of the planet's ecosystems, conducted between 2001 and 2005] estimates that between one quarter and one third of the total number of known plant species – that is, 60,000 to 100,000 species – are threatened with extinction.'

Seed banks must contend with two very different types of seeds in trying to save plants for posterity. Orthodox seeds, which are produced by 70 to 80 per cent of plants, can tolerate drying. They

Entrance to the underground seed vault at Kew's Millennium
Seed Bank, which is designed to last for 500 years

tend to be small and are programmed to linger in the environment before they germinate. The MSBP dries and freezes orthodox seeds at minus 20°C, slowing down their metabolism, while keeping them alive. Drying the seeds is necessary before freezing them, otherwise any water they still contain would turn to ice, rupturing the seeds' cells and causing germination to fail.

Recalcitrant seeds, as they are known, which make up the remaining 20 to 30 per cent, are harder to store. They tend to be larger, with thin outer coats and a predisposition to germinate rapidly. Plants with recalcitrant seeds often live in wetter habitats such as tropical rainforests, but oaks and horse chestnuts are recalcitrant too. If you dry such seeds, you kill them. Instead, the MSBP's scientists must carefully cut out part of each seed's embryo, treat it with a chemical to stop ice crystallisation and then store it in liquid nitrogen at minus 196°C. When the embryo is coaxed into life, it is provided with a food source to replace that usually provided by the seed or its environment.

Seeds can live for a remarkably long time. One of the most ancient known to have germinated was a date palm seed from Masada, Israel, which at the time was 2,000 years old. The oldest seeds that the MSBP has managed to grow had been shed from their parent plant 200 years earlier. They were collected in 1803 from the Dutch East India Company Gardens in South Africa by a Dutch merchant, Jan Teerlink. He tucked forty folded paper packets of them into a red leather wallet before boarding the *Henriette*, anchored at Cape Town. The ship was bound for the Netherlands but was captured by the British before reaching its destination. Although Teerlink was released, the British seized the ship's cargo and papers, including the wallet of seeds, and sent them to the Tower of London. They were later moved to the Public Records Office near to Kew where they remained until rediscovered by a Dutch researcher in 2005. When scientists tried to grow a sample of the seeds, they were rewarded by the germination of a *Liparia villosa*, a *Leucospermum conocarpodendron* and an *Acacia* species. The *Acacia* and the *Leucospermum* survive today, the latter now a healthy bush around a metre high.

The oldest seeds in the MSPB's vault are around forty years old. The scientists test a sample from each banked species every ten years to ensure they are still able to germinate. They also conduct 'accelerated ageing' experiments to ascertain the longevity of different seeds. This involves rehydrating them and subjecting them to conditions of stress such as high levels of both humidity and temperature. The method generates a 'seed survival curve', showing how many seeds of the species in question are likely to germinate at given times in the future. The forecast longevity of a seed sample can then be compared with the known longevity of marker species under the same conditions.

'That's been done with many agricultural species,' says Smith. 'Sugar beet seeds under those conditions are forecast to last for 10,000 years, while lettuce ones last for only a few hundred. We're very lucky because most seeds of the crops we rely on are long lived. However, some seeds are comparatively short lived; we're working out why and what we need to look out for. Temperate species with small embryos tend to be shorter lived, for example, so they will live for decades rather than thousands of years.'

Knowing the quality and longevity of seeds is vital if they are to be put to good use in the real world. The Ecoseed project is investigating the influence on seed quality of climatic variability during crop growth. The team has begun examining the effects of withholding water from fields of sunflowers and is starting to investigate the germination ability, size and longevity of seeds produced from those crops. 'It could be that those environmental

Over two billion seeds are stored in glass jars in the seed vault.
The oldest are now forty years old

changes will affect one of the inherent properties of the seeds that we can bank,' explains Hugh Pritchard, Head of Research at the MSBP's Seed Conservation Department. 'It could be that we're in for a nasty surprise; that actually the seeds store less well as a result of climate change.'

The impact of climate change on plants can be difficult to forecast. General predictions have suggested that species living on mountains will have to migrate to higher altitudes if they are to continue growing in the environmental conditions to which they are acclimatised. As a result they will face a decline as, eventually, there will be nowhere higher for them to go. However, Kew's studies of the wild grapevines (*Vitis vinifera* subspecies *sylvestris*) in Sardinia suggest that plants growing at the highest altitudes are less likely to be affected than those a few hundred metres down the mountainsides. This is because vine seeds need a cold spell in winter in order to break their dormancy. If temperatures do not drop sufficiently, the seeds will not germinate, reducing the likelihood of their natural emergence in the spring. Higher up the mountain, the temperatures are still sufficiently low for the cold spell to occur.

With climate change, deforestation and urbanisation all affecting the world's ecosystems, an important role for Kew is to help restore degraded habitats to their former biodiversity. One example is a project that Kew has carried out with a wide range of partners. Fifteen hundred years ago, huarango (*Prosopis limensis*) trees kept the soil of the Ica Valley in one of the world's driest deserts fertile and moist, while providing forage and food to eat. Their exceptionally long roots (sometimes over 50 metres) are able to tap deep groundwater, making their survival possible in arid environments. In pre-Columbian Nazca times, the trees prevented erosion, while

Planting huarango trees in Peru

their canopy ameliorated the extreme desert temperatures. But then the Nazca were driven to cut them down to clear land for agriculture. When the clearance reached a critical threshold, the fragile ecosystem failed, leaving the Nazca at the mercy of El Niño floods and fierce desert winds.

For a long time, the ancestral paths that the Nazca traced in the desert sands were all that was left of their once rich civilisation. Today, however, the Ica Valley's huarango forest is rising again. Scientists from Kew's team in Peru developed protocols required to germinate huarango seeds and associated forest species, shared this knowledge with local communities and established a plant nursery within the Faculty of Agronomy at the National University of Ica (UNICA). The 10,000 or so native tree and shrub seedlings produced by the nursery each year are breathing new life back into the desert and helping provide food, timber and fuel for the Ica Valley's current 700,000 inhabitants.

Seeds can provide some surprising insights into past ecosystems, which can be useful when trying to restore habitats. Although those habitats may have changed over time, plants evolve only slowly, so the characteristics exhibited in seeds relate to ecosystems that may have existed tens of thousands of years ago.

The agents that seeds use for dispersal can be particularly important to consider in restoration projects. Take *Rafflesia*, for example. This plant, which grows in the rainforests of South-East Asia, is well known for having the biggest flower in the world. However, the plant's grapefruit-sized, fleshy fruits, which can be 15 centimetres across, are less well understood.

'I'd never read in the literature about what disperses the fruit,' says Wolfgang Stuppy. 'Someone had written that they thought it was rodents, as they had seen them nibbling the fruit. However, although you get all kinds of animals feeding on fruits, it doesn't mean they are the disperser. I read that the *Rafflesia* fruit has a pulp that smells yeasty, which is characteristic of fruits you see in elephant territories in Africa. Mammals such as elephants don't see colours well but have a very acute sense of smell, so I immediately realised that the fruit was designed to be dispersed by the Asian elephant. This elephant is an extremely endangered species and hardly present any more in the habitats where you find *Rafflesia*. To restore such environments, you either have to intervene and be a gardener for as long as you want the species to exist, or you get the animal back.'

This is not as far-reaching an idea as it might at first sound. When scientists in Africa examined areas from which elephants have now disappeared, their findings showed that plant populations that had been reliant on elephants to disperse their seeds had shrunk as a result. Elephant-dispersed fruits generally have little flesh and a big stone too large to be eaten by any other animal. The fruits of *Balanites aegyptiaca* trees, also known as the desert date, are an example. The researchers found that germination of *Balanites* seeds was reduced by 95 per cent when elephants were not present.

Although a small percentage of undispersed *Balanites* seeds will germinate in the absence of elephants, the seedlings have a survival rate of just 16 per cent. It seems that only bush elephants provide this rare tree with a highly effective dispersal service that guarantees the regeneration of existing populations and possibly also the establishment of new ones. The research demonstrates the devastating impact that hindering a plant's seed-dispersal mechanism can have.

Stuppy adds the final word: 'The seed is the only phase in the plant's life when it can travel, so it's a crucial moment in that life. This is why seeds have all these extraordinary adaptations to help them get around, whether by wind, water, animals or humans.'

20

A USEFUL WEED

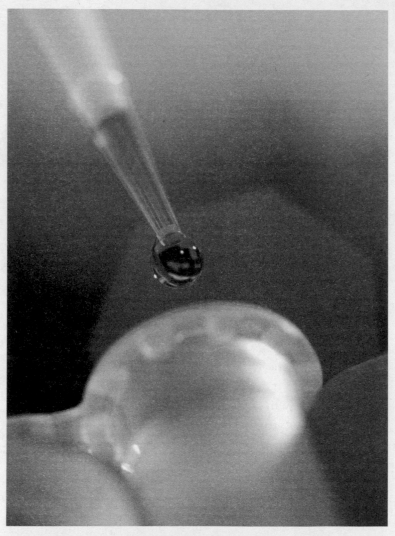

A sample of plant DNA is prepared for analysis

AT A GLANCE, *Arabidopsis thaliana* seems little more than a minute flowering weed. But this nondescript bit of greenery has become a Rosetta Stone for plant genetics. In 2000 it was the first plant to have its genome fully sequenced, by which we mean that all of the DNA in its chromosomes was analysed.

This deciphering of its genetic material has provided insights into the molecular processes that take place in cells, underpinning many plant traits, whilst also revealing vital pointers on how they might be controlled. Specifically, *Arabidopsis* research has become a bedrock for genetically modified (GM) crops, as scientists have discovered how to introduce new characteristics in a quicker and more targeted way than via traditional plant breeding.

The star of this green revolution is a plant as unassuming as the peas Mendel examined for his groundbreaking, nineteenth-century work on plant inheritance (as explained in Chapter 10). Commonly known as wall cress or mouse-ear cress, *Arabidopsis thaliana* grows widely across a variety of terrains. Native to Europe, Asia and north-western Africa, it is a member of the mustard (Brassicaceae) family, which includes cultivated species such as cabbage and radish. You can find it on rocky ground, dunes and in other sandy spots, as well as on waste ground or other disturbed habitats such as railway lines.

Its shifting name is a good reflection of how plant naming conventions have changed over the last few hundred years. The German physician Johannes Thal first described the plant in 1577 in the heavily wooded Harz Mountains of northern Germany, and Carl Linnaeus named it *Arabis thaliana* in his honour. Then in 1842, German botanist Gustav Heynhold placed it in a newly delineated genus, *Arabidopsis*, which took its name from the Greek for 'resembling *Arabis*'.

In 1907, the German scientist Friedrich Laibach correctly observed that the plant has just five chromosomes (others had miscounted, giving it only three), which was the lowest odd number known at that time for any plant. Despite this discovery, Laibach was disappointed by *Arabidopsis* because the genetic content of its cells was small and he was looking for a plant with many more chromosomes to study. So for the next thirty years he turned his attention elsewhere, only returning to *Arabidopsis* in 1937.

In 1943 Laibach suggested that *Arabidopsis thaliana* would make a model organism for the scientific study of flowering plants, based on factors such as its quick growing time (just six weeks from germination to the production of seeds) and the ease with which it created hybrids and mutations. In 1945 his student Erna Reinholz wrote her PhD thesis on the *Arabidopsis* mutants she generated, using the technique of X-ray mutagenesis (something that at the time smacked of science fiction), exposing the plants to X-rays and in doing so changing the genetic material of their cells, thereby creating mutants.

Her mutants included late-flowering plants derived from early-flowering ones, a pioneering example of genetic tinkering that was later developed for GM crops. Curiously, it was the US military that was responsible for the dissemination and full publication of Reinholz's thesis. They latched on to it because the phrase '*Röntgen-Mutationen*' (meaning X-ray mutation) in its title had attracted analysts looking for evidence of a German atomic bomb programme.

In the 1950s and 1960s, work by geneticists John Langridge and George Rédei further highlighted the credentials of *Arabidopsis* for modelling plant genetics, in the face of rival proposals for plants such as the petunia or the tomato. But there were multiple reasons for *A. thaliana* having bagged the leading role in plant genetics research, similar to that played by mice and fruit flies (*Drosophila*) in animal research.

First, the wide geographical range and diversity of *Arabidopsis* made it perfect for investigating how it adapts to its environment. It is also a rapid grower and, because of its miniature size, it is ideally suited to growth in laboratory conditions. At a more technical level, *A. thaliana* meets the requirements of microscopic analysis, the relative translucency of its young seedlings and their roots a boon for live cell imaging.

The plant's relatively small genome makes it an easier candidate than others for genetic analysis, with the latest estimate putting the size of the *Arabidopsis* genome – technically known as its C-value – at 157 megabase pairs (Mb). Base pairs is the unit of measurement used for DNA, referring to its two stranded, 'double helix' structure, which requires pairing of its component parts. It was initially thought to have the smallest genome of any flowering plant, although that title has now passed to a carnivorous plant, *Genlisea margaretae*, which has as a C-value less than half the size of that of *Arabidopsis*. By contrast, the largest genome currently known is that belonging to the spectacular but rare Japanese flowering beauty *Paris japonica*, with a C-value of 148,880 Mb – over 948 times as big as that of *Arabidopsis*. 'It's so large that when stretched out it would be taller than Big Ben,' says plant geneticist Ilia Leitch of Kew's Jodrell Laboratory.

Advances during the 1980s confirmed *Arabidopsis* as a model organism. In 1983, the first detailed genetic map of the plant was published, followed three years later by the first section of the *Arabidopsis* gene sequence. Experiments conducted later in the decade demonstrated that *A. thaliana* was particularly amenable to the transfer of genes using a specially tailored bacterium (*Agrobacterium tumefaciens*). This is a naturally occurring soil bacterium that has been genetically modified to carry specific DNA and used to infect a plant, which then takes the DNA into its own genome. By 1989, the first transfer of a DNA segment containing a mutant gene was helping ease the way towards the controlled genetic manipulation of plants.

The use of modified *Agrobacterium tumefaciens*, which causes crown-gall disease in plants is one of the main methods for transferring DNA to a plant in the creation of GM crops, using a technique with the rather charming name 'floral-dip'. This involves dipping a flower into a solution of modified *Agrobacterium*, containing the particular DNA of interest, and a detergent. Fluorescent markers can also be introduced, which allow researchers to trace the developmental progress of the inserted DNA in the gene sequence.

The other main method used to insert DNA into a plant relies on what is sometimes called a gene gun or, more technically, a 'biolistic particle delivery system'. Invented in the 1980s, it relies on an adapted air pistol to blast metal particles coated with a relevant gene into the cells of the target plant. It sounds simple if messy, but initial tests on onion cells (chosen as a good test target because of their large size) showed it works, with the onions soon displaying the characteristics of their newly inserted gene.

With the science and technology still evolving, the first GM crops appeared in the 1980s, led by tobacco plants modified variously to resist antibiotics, herbicides and pests. Today, GM variants

Cotton, genetically-modified variants of which grow
around the world today

growing around the world include crops such as potato, corn, maize, tomato, soya and cotton. But despite having been in use for three decades, GM crops still spark heated debate.

In the meantime, scientists are continuing to seek answers to basic questions about why certain plants have much larger genomes than others, with the largest believed to be about 2,000 times bigger than the smallest. One mystery is the lack of correlation between a plant's ploidy levels – the number of sets of chromosomes in each of its cells (as discussed in Chapter 12) – and its genome size (the amount of DNA in its chromosomes). Big increases in ploidy levels do not necessarily result in similar increases in genome size. 'Some plants have genomes thirty times larger than our own,' says Leitch. 'But a plant with the highest ploidy levels, such as the Mexican stonecrop *Sedum suaveolens*, which is eighty-ploid, has a rather small genome size.'

Understanding the relationships between plant genome size and how it affects the plant has vital practical outcomes. 'Some people may wonder whether it really matters whether one organism has more DNA than another. The answer is a resounding "yes",' says Leitch. 'Consequences operate at all levels from the cell up to the whole organism and beyond.'

Kew is a leader in plant genome research, as well as being custodian of a crucial global database detailing the genome sizes of thousands of species worldwide. When first set up at Kew in 2001, the Plant DNA C-Values Database carried data for 3,864 species. The latest version, updated in 2012, contains 8,510 species. Plant geneticists can combine widespread information on genomes with insights gained from *Arabidopsis* to try to puzzle out which genes do what and how.

Another area explored by Kew researchers, using experimental data derived from studies of *Arabidopsis*, includes the effects of moisture and temperature on seed storage to identify short- and long-lived plant seeds. Understanding how seed dormancy works at molecular levels will help refine the methods used for crop planting and plant conservation work, particularly that aimed at restoring habitats. Analysis of how genes in *Arabidopsis* affect the range of the plant's flowering times has, meanwhile, helped researchers use genetic manipulation to create plants with a much longer range of flowering times.

How plants achieve disease resistance is another vital element of global food production. Here, genetic studies have shed valuable light on the interaction between plants and disease-causing pathogens. For example, tests on *Arabidopsis* were used to show which genes gave some plants resistance to *Blumeria graminis*, responsible for powdery mildew in grasses. Identifying which genes were involved has allowed researchers to target them in an effort to create variants that could resist the mildew.

Plant hormones have also been important in crop improvement. In the 1950s, American plant geneticist Norman Borlaug used traditional breeding techniques to create new varieties of dwarf wheat, which produced high yields at the expense of stem growth (as described in Chapter 16). Introduced around the world during the 1960s and 1970s, Borlaug's extra-productive dwarf wheats were credited with saving many lives.

Later on, research based on studies of *Arabidopsis* pinpointed the precise mechanism by which the repression of a particular plant hormone called gibberellin created such high-yield dwarf wheats. Further research, using models derived from *Arabidopsis*, is now shedding light on how the manipulation of relevant genes may help create crops suitable for some of the harsher environments appearing as a result of global climate change. The number of saline environments, for example, is increasing around the world

Zea mays, maize, another species to which GM plant technology
has been applied

Saintpaulia teitensis, a rare endemic African violet, known only to a single hillside in Kenya. It is threatened with extinction, together with a quarter to a third of all known plant species

Savannah habitat, Laikipia, Kenya, with *Acacia drepanolobium* (the whistling thorn tree) in the foreground

Seed collecting in Burkina Faso, West Africa, sometimes involves climbing and catching. Kew's Millennium Seed Bank Partnership aims to bank seeds from 25% of the world's plants by 2020, prioritising those that are endemic, endangered and economically valuable

Madagascar's striking *Tahina spectabilis*, a new palm found in 2006, previously completely unknown to science. Approximately 2,000 new species of plants are still being discovered each year

Pressing plants in the field on an expedition to Mali. Over 30,000 specimens are sent back to Kew each year from all around the world

Collecting seeds of *Sesamum abbreviatum*, a plant exclusive to the Namibian desert

Rainforests, such as this one in Sabah, South-East Asia, provide one of the most species-rich environments

Arid landscape and dry river bed, Bahia, Brazil. One of the biggest environmental risks facing humankind today is climate change

Yams are a major food source in tropical and sub-tropical regions but tend to be overlooked in favour of grain crops. With impending global challenges of climate change and population increase, they may prove to be useful alternatives to crops that require significantly more water

Cultivation of rice in Madagascar

In Europe and the USA there has been a dramatic decline in bee numbers. As pollinators, bees are vital to agriculture. Kew scientists are undertaking biochemical research to understand better what attracts them to flowers and how they can be encouraged to become more efficient pollinators

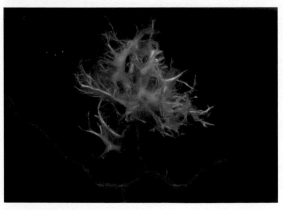

Plants and fungi engage in mutually beneficial relationships, the most important of which are mycorrhizae, where fungi live on and in a plant's roots. Both depend on this to develop and thrive. It is estimated that as many as 90% of all plants depend on mycorrhizae to survive

as a result of agricultural practices and shifts in climate and sea levels. Developing crops able to handle salty conditions is a current challenge for researchers, with *Arabidopsis* studies being used to work out which genes affect the saline tolerance of different species.

New techniques are also being developed for creating GM crops, of which one of the most recent has been dubbed GM editing. This involves applying genetic modifications to plants in ways that might happen naturally, rather than simply inserting 'foreign' genes – an approach that could be viewed as merely giving Nature a push, rather than applying what opponents of GM see as a distortion.

If this twenty-first-century approach to analysing *Arabidopsis thaliana* sounds like space-age science, that is entirely appropriate, given that it was the first plant to undergo its complete life cycle in space, from seed germination to flowering and setting seed, when grown on board the Mir Space Station in 1997. And further tests are planned by the US space agency NASA, which intends to grow *Arabidopsis* on the International Space Station in 2015.

The aim will be to determine which genes are activated – or in some way controlled – by gravity. Staff at NASA believe this could have practical applications back on earth, in terms of our greater understanding of root and shoot architecture, as well as revealing how plants adjust their growth in space. And if humans are to colonise other planets in the future, our success may well owe a great deal to research undertaken on a tiny plant that has made a huge mark.

21

A BLOOMING TREE
OF LIFE

Amborella trichopoda, which is known from DNA analysis to
represent an early evolutionary line of flowering plants.
By Alice Tangerini from the Shirley Sherwood Collection

KEW'S EMBLEM, BENEATH the royal coat of arms, is a flower. Nothing surprising about that, you might think. But why not a fern? Or a conifer? Or even a fungus? All of these have been around far longer than flowers.

Flowers are earth's youngsters. They've been here for perhaps no more than 140–180 million years, with the first fossils dating back just 139 million years. In evolutionary terms, this puts them still in short trousers; seed plants appeared a full 230 million years earlier, and the very first land plants another 100 million before that.

But, once they'd made their appearance, these gaudy newcomers swept aside all before them and went on to become amazingly successful. Within 70 million years of their first appearance, flowering plants had attained ecological supremacy in a majority of habitats and over a wide geographical area. Today, flowering plants (known botanically as angiosperms) are the dominant group of plants on earth. There are 457 families and approximately 350,000 species, compared to roughly 10,000 species of spore-producing plants such as ferns, and 750 species of non-flowering plants (gymnosperms) such as conifers.

From the earliest botanical musings, there has been a long-running fascination with how different plants relate to each other:

how they evolved, when and in what order. As we have learned in earlier chapters, for most of scientific history, evidence for piecing together these family relationships among flowers was collected by the simple but reliable method of looking at them. This involved counting the various parts present, taking careful note of characteristics such as shape, size and colour, and then comparing similarities and differences between different plants' flowers. This principle of classification by observation is known as 'morphology'.

Illustrating this principle, the 'Plant Family Beds' are tucked away in one of the loveliest and most private corners of Kew, behind high brick walls that protect and shield the plantings. This area was originally laid out as a botanic garden in 1846 by William Hooker, when he was Director of Kew. And it was here that the relationships between different plant families, as determined by the Victorian botanists, were displayed for public and scientists alike.

The walled area had previously been used as a kitchen garden to supply the royal household, but on the orders of Queen Victoria it was placed at the disposal of Kew. William Hooker originally used a scientific classification known as the Natural System, devised by the French botanist Antoine Laurent de Jussieu, to label the Kew plants, arranging his plantings in informal, irregularly shaped beds. By 1869 the walled garden had been reorganised by George Bentham and Joseph Hooker, William's son, on more overtly scientific principles. Reflecting this more precise arrangement, they gave it a new name: the Order Beds.

Bentham and Hooker Junior, who represented all that is best in Victorian botany, set about their task methodically and with typical thoroughness. The painstaking process of categorising all the flowering plants, and devising a new system of classification to describe them, took over twenty years. They arranged the plants

The Plant Family Beds at Kew, c.1900.
Formerly called the Order Beds, plants are arranged according to
their evolutionary relationships

in long straight flower beds so they could show people how the system worked. It was a brilliant idea; education was always an important part of their vision. Over the same period, the specimens in the Herbarium were also reorganised according to the same principles.

Bentham and Hooker followed the much earlier work of the naturalist John Ray, who had established the grand division of the flowering plants into 'monocotyledon' and 'dicotyledon': that is, plants that produce one ('mono-') or two ('di-') seed leaves from the germinating seed (the 'cotyledon'). To this Bentham and Hooker added one further grouping: the 'gymnosperm', or non-flowering plant. Within these three large ranked groups, they identified 202 separate families.

Their classification was based on close examination of the morphology of the flowering plants – in other words, their structure and appearance: petals, stamens and leaves, as well as other vegetative parts. Bentham and Hooker's taxonomy (the analysis of a plant's characteristics for the purpose of classification) was highly practical because they chose such clear characteristics to define each family, which made their system extremely popular. It continued to be used at Kew for the next hundred years, even though many different competing taxonomies were produced elsewhere, both in Britain and abroad.

Each new taxonomy sought to modify the work that had gone before, hoping to provide a better and more 'natural' way of organising the flowering plant families, making it more useful to botanists both in the herbarium and in the field. Of course, the old morphological techniques had their limits. Using processes based primarily on similarity of appearance caused some significant problems for taxonomists, particularly when trying to reconstruct an evolutionary family tree. The problem was that, just as with human families, some closely related plants did not look at all alike, while plants that had evolved independently to look similar, perhaps because they shared an environmental or ecological niche, were not, in fact, closely related at all.

Morphological classification to this day remains vitally important out in the field, where researchers need to be able to make subtle distinctions and identify patterns of variation on sight, allowing them to differentiate and detect species, as well as other higher taxonomic categories. Here, where a hand lens and a great knowledge of the physical characteristics of plants are invaluable, we owe the patient Victorians much. However, as so often in science, a long-standing orthodoxy eventually needs updating. As the twenty-first century approached plant taxonomy was in need of a breakthrough.

It came in the early 1990s. An international group of botanists, co-headed by Kew's Jodrell Laboratory, began to explore the possibilities of making a completely different kind of classification, based on the new science of DNA sequencing. They aimed to determine whether genetic analysis might yield a better way to classify plants, by focusing on the molecular nature of the plant, rather than solely on its appearance. As Mark Chase, Keeper of the Jodrell Laboratory, explains, 'We didn't, in fact, set out to change anything, just to evaluate how well DNA would work as a tool for examining relationships of plants, suspecting rather that it might not. It turned out to be ideal, but we certainly didn't know that when we started.'

The Angiosperm Phylogeny Group (APG), an informal network of botanists, came together in the mid-1990s with the purpose of using the results of DNA sequencing to produce a new family classification for the flowering plants, in which all relationships would be based on how closely related plants were, as defined by the amount of genetic (DNA) difference between species. Along the way, this also gave the group the chance to check how well existing classifications reflected their findings. And the results were intriguing. The group compared its own family tree to those of classifiers such as Bentham and Hooker, as well as to those of later stalwarts of the field, such as the American taxonomist Arthur Cronquist. They looked for a percentage of 'concordance', meaning the number of families in an older classification that were confirmed by their new system.

Bentham and Hooker, the APG results suggested, had been for the most part right in their classification, based on what could be seen by the naked eye and the microscope alone. Mark Chase takes up the story. 'We began seeing results at the family level that were fairly good, with 87 per cent concordance about which families should be recognised.' So Bentham and Hooker had managed to correctly place almost 90 per cent of plant families, using only the plant morphology. This was an impressive result, given that the classification had been established in the nineteenth century with minimal technology. Chase continues, 'But among the other 10 per cent that were not in accord were some pretty spectacular cases where they had got things wrong. And what didn't match well in particular were the higher taxonomic categories (the major groupings), such as orders; there, the correspondence was almost zero.' One example of wrong placement was the case of Paeoniaceae – the peony family. The peonies had always been classified as members or close relatives of the buttercup family, Ranunculaceae, due to their possession of many shared characteristics: the similarity of their flowers, for example.

Yet DNA analysis by the Angiosperm Phylogeny Group revealed that peonies are in actual fact more closely related to the saxifrages and stonecrops, several rows away in Bentham and Hooker's scheme for the Order Beds. So, the poor old peonies in the beds were duly dug up and moved. The APG's ideas were a big 'ask' for the world of plant science to accept, requiring huge shifts in the story of flowering plants. It was far from just being a question of naming. APG's new 'family tree' demanded that plant biologists accept a substantial rewriting of the history of these plants.

Chemistry helped in the reordering, too. The APG classification puts many families that were not previously thought to be closely related into the order Brassicales. According to one earlier, widely admired system, invented by Arthur Cronquist, the ten families that now make up Brassicales would have been placed in five orders in two subclasses. However, chemical analysis revealed that these plants all produce 'mustard oils', the natural compounds that give pungent plants such as broccoli, cabbage

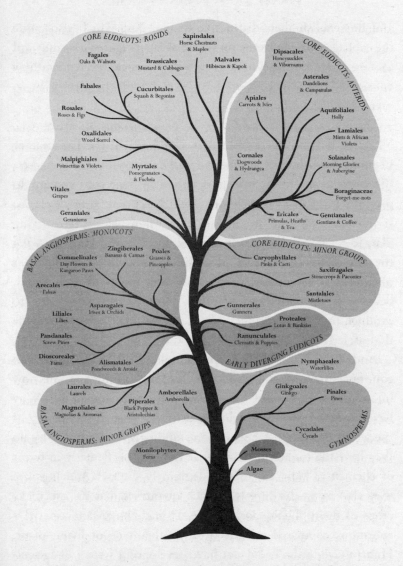

This tree of plant evolution shows current thinking of the
relationships between the major groups of plants

and horseradish their distinctive flavour, and which also guide the cabbage white butterfly on where to lay its eggs. These mustard oils are produced in plant cells by a biochemical mechanism now considered too complex to have evolved independently in so many families.

Having a plant family tree is of enormous practical use. Nitrogen fixation, for example, is a property of the Fabaceae or Leguminosae, the pea and bean family, where the plants harvest the work of micro-organisms that live in their root systems to produce a supply of this element, which is essential to all plants. If scientists want to investigate the origins of nitrogen-fixing plants, they will be greatly helped by a family tree showing the closest living relatives possessing the same properties. 'It's obviously a very important phenomenon for us to understand, because if we could enable other plant species to be able to produce their own nitrogen, then we wouldn't have to provide that as fertiliser,' says Chase.

And, just as in Bentham and Hooker's day, foci of research continue to evolve and develop. 'One of the things we are now interested in,' enthuses Chase, 'is what is underlying all this. Why have flowering plants, which appeared very late in the history of the world, nonetheless been so outstandingly successful? Why do they have the interesting traits that they do, particularly in terms of chemistry? Why are they so extremely diverse? And how are they able to produce seeds in such quantities that we can make crops of them? The quantity of seeds made by an angiosperm is enormous compared to that of any other type of living plant. Human civilisation could not have developed a system of agriculture solely based on the seeds of gymnosperms or the spores of ferns – they are simply not productive enough. It's really bizarre in the history of the planet to find a group of plants capable of being so productive that they can sustain a population of 7 billion people.'

For Chase, plants are not all work. His office in the Jodrell Laboratory boasts a rainbow of orchids and other plants along its shelves and windowsills. 'I'm a big plant nerd . . . Flowering plants have had the evolutionary capacity to take over the face of the planet in a very short space of evolutionary time, and do these amazing things – actively trapping insects and being carnivorous, for example. Flowering plants do such incredibly marvellous things!'

Like Bentham and Hooker, scientists today still need their capacity for wonder.

22

DYNAMIC
RAINFOREST

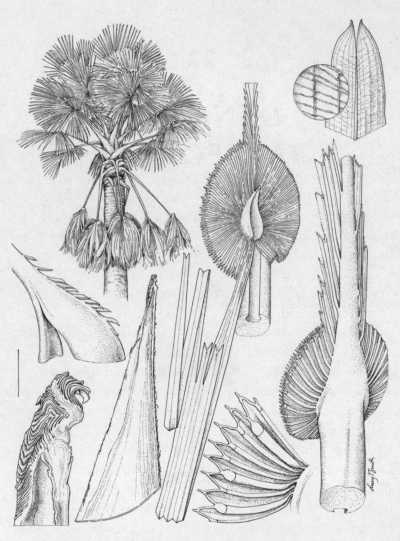

Madagascar's *Tahina spectabilis*, a new palm found in 2006, drawn by Lucy T. Smith

IN LATE 2006, just as botanists were finalising a state-of-the-art scientific account of the palm family, news emerged of an extraordinary find. French plantation manager Xavier Metz was walking with his family in a remote part of north-western Madagascar when he saw a huge palm tree with a striking candelabra of yellow flowers. It turned out that despite its huge dimensions – it stands 18 metres high and its fan-shaped leaves span 5 metres – the tree was completely unknown to science. When specimens of this palm eventually arrived in the UK from Madagascar, Kew's former Head of Palm Research, John Dransfield, realised that it represented not only a new species but also a new genus, *Tahina*.

'Initially someone sent me an email with six or seven pictures and suggested I take a look,' explains Dransfield, who is now retired but remains an Honorary Research Associate at Kew. 'It looked exactly like the talipot palm (*Corypha umbraculifera*) from India and Sri Lanka, which is a huge fan palm. However, it was in the wrong place; you never get *Corypha* in Madagascar. I got very excited and contacted Xavier Metz who sent more pictures. I realised it had to be something else. A close colleague in Madagascar, Mijoro Rakotoarinivo, was able to make the first specimen collection. In April 2007 he was coming to the UK to finish off his PhD with me at Kew. We had the greatest excitement over Easter. I opened up the box he brought containing the specimens and realised it was a member of the Chuniophoeniceae tribe (a tribe is a taxonomic rank between family and genus), at the time, of three genera: *Kerriodoxa*, *Chuniophoenix* and *Nannorrhops*.

'*Tahina* is humongous; it's a very, very big palm, and only inhabits Madagascar. *Kerriodoxa* is a palm of the low mountainous and wet forests of Phuket Island and the neighbouring parts of southern Thailand; *Chuniophoenix* is a small forest undergrowth palm that lives in China and Vietnam; and *Nannorrhops* is a desert palm from Arabia, Afghanistan and Pakistan. So what on earth joins these four genera together? Well, it's the structure of the inflorescence [the complete flower head of a plant] where the flowers are held. This is how I was able to say when I opened the box that it had to be a member of Chuniophoeniceae. And when one of my clever students looked at its molecular make-up, they agreed that, indeed, the only place it could possibly go is in that tribe.'

Dransfield, Rakotoarinivo and their colleagues named it *Tahina spectabilis*. *Tahina* is Malagasy for 'to be blessed', as well as being the name of one of Metz's daughter's, while *spectabilis* is Latin for 'spectacular'.

Tahina spectabilis is one in a long line of new finds of palm species and genera that have been uncovered by Kew botanists since the 1980s. When the first edition of *Genera Palmarum: The Evolution and Classification of Palms* was published in 1987, it detailed 200 genera and 2,700 species of palms. But by the time the second edition finally went to press in mid-2008, including the last-minute addition of *Tahina spectabilis*, its authors had classified 2,500 species in 183 genera. The decrease in species numbers resulted from rigorous work, which revealed some species that were initially thought to be distinct, to be variants of other species. (Joseph Hooker would have been proud of such lumping.) However, a significant number of the total comprises entirely new species that have been described since 1987. Advances in the use of genetic tools for classifying flowering plants lie at the heart of the huge strides made in our understanding of the palm family, enabling experts in that field to create a DNA-based 'tree of life' for them. The new classification reflects the history of the family and traces the evolutionary paths that have led to the current distributions of palms across the world.

When most people think of palms, they bring to mind the iconic trees of tropical coastal sunsets or hardy species, such as *Trachycarpus fortunei*, widely used in British gardens. However, palms, which belong to the family of flowering plants called Arecaceae, are extremely diverse. A stroll around Kew's Palm House, which contains 249 species of palm, gives a good insight into the many sizes, leaf shapes and colours of the family.

The largest living specimen at Kew is *Attalea butyracea* or 'babassu', which has a tall, stout trunk topped by a crown of fronds, and is necessarily located in the lofty centre of the glasshouse. However, its leaves are beginning to reach the curved apex. Its nearby relatives include: *Kerriodoxa elegans*, which has large fan-shaped leaves atop a relatively short stem; *Pinanga densiflora*, characterised by clusters of stems with mottled leaves; *Astrocaryum mexicanum*, a pale-stemmed palm with evil-looking black spines (Palm House Manager Scott Taylor has scars to prove their skin-piercing capabilities); and *Hyophorbe lagenicaulis*, an elegant bottle palm with a wide, swollen base to its golden-brown stem.

Taylor has the task of ensuring that a wide variety of palms are on display, in good health, and that there is a replacement for the babassu when it finally becomes too high for the glasshouse roof

The largest living palm at Kew, the 'babassu',
Attalea butyracea

and has to be cut down. A vigorous-looking specimen of *Elaeis guineensis*, or African oil palm, is a possible contender.

Taylor explains how such shifts are done. 'If we were to move this palm,' he says, pointing to the large oil palm, whose saw-edged leaves, 10 centimetres wide, grow from its base, 'I'd give it about half a metre either side, trench it down one side [a process that involves cutting through the roots, digging a trench and filling it with organic matter to help new roots form], give it time to heal, then do the next side and so on. It can take a number of months but then you have a nice dense root ball. We'd also reduce the leaves because if you damage the roots, you need to balance that by removing some of the leaves.'

There are plenty of new palms waiting to fill any spaces that become available; *Veitchia subdisticha* is another that would benefit from more room, a palm that only grows wild in the Solomon Islands and is commonly known as a stilt palm because of the shape of its roots.

Kew's living palm collection played a vital role in the recent reclassification process. DNA extracted from the plants was used to help build up the family tree of palm life. The subsequent genetic work identified five evolutionary lineages that are recognised in the new classification by five subfamilies: Calamoideae, Nypoideae, Coryphoideae, Ceroxyloideae and Arecoideae. The Calamoideae comprises twenty-one genera of mostly spiny palms, including the vine-like rattans commonly used for making furniture. The Nypoideae has just a single genus and species, that of the mangrove palm (*Nypa fruticans*), which grows in Asia's swamps. Coryphoideae, with forty-six genera, is primarily made up of the fan palm subfamily, although it also encompasses some palms with different leaf shapes, such as the date palm (*Phoenix*). Ceroxyloideae has eight genera of varying characteristics; and Arecoideae is the largest subfamily with 107 genera, containing well-known palms such as the coconut and oil palm.

'We completely rearranged the subfamilies,' explains Bill Baker, Assistant Keeper of Kew's Herbarium and a palm taxonomist.

We had major shocks, such as whole groups of palms with feather-shaped leaves being found to be derived from the fan-palm group. Although, at a practical level, a lot of the genera have remained unchanged, the whole evolutionary structure within the palms has been overhauled.

In the past, inferences about how palms are related and about how they should be classified were based on intuition, as well as on traditional untested assumptions.

That was the situation across all organisms, not just plants. People accepted and understood evolution but didn't have an objective way to try to unpick the stories it told, short of studying the fossil record. But DNA sequences are themselves a kind of amazing fossil record. They show mutations that have accumulated in genomes over millions of years and persisted. Some get overwritten and there is some conflict and confusion, but that signal is, in a sense, a molecular fossil record.

Today, palm diversity has a rather uneven global distribution. Almost 1,000 species live on the islands clustered between the Malay peninsula and New Guinea; the Americas have 730 species and Madagascar 199; but the vast continent of Africa possesses just 65 species. The greatest diversity of palms is found within hot, humid tropical rainforests; only a few live in arid climes.

All flowering plants, including the palms, are known to have first appeared during the Cretaceous period, which began around

Date palm grove in Oman

145 million years ago. Using the new genetic techniques, Baker and his colleagues were able to show that the diversification that resulted in today's palms began during the mid-Cretaceous period, around 100 million years ago. Their analyses of how the geographic range of palms evolved suggest that the most likely distribution of the most recent common ancestor of palms was centred in Central and North America and Eurasia.

Botanists have long pondered how rainforests originated. Alfred Russel Wallace was one of the earliest naturalists to address the question, after travelling in the Brazilian Amazon in the mid-nineteenth century. He came to the conclusion, after studying the area's rainforest plants and animals in detail, that the 'great mass of the equatorial forests' must have benefited from consistent climatic conditions over time, whereas earth's temperate areas had experienced periodic checks and extinctions. He wrote in his 1878 book, *Tropical Nature, and Other Essays*:

> In one evolution has had a fair chance; in the other, it has had countless difficulties thrown in its way. The equatorial regions are then, as regards their past and present life history, a more ancient world than that represented by the temperate zones, a world in which the laws that have governed the progressive development of life have operated with comparatively little check for countless ages, and have resulted in those infinitely varied and beautiful forms.

Kew's research shows that palm evolution conforms to a pattern of constant diversification. If you use palms as proxies for rainforest ecosystems, this is in line with Wallace's original hypothesis that gradual evolution has caused the richness of species to be found in rainforests today. This is despite the fact that we now know that rainforests are very dynamic places that have been subjected to significant climatic changes over time. Another study also supports the idea that diversity has come about through evolutionary changes over very long periods. Scientists from Stony Brook University, USA, discovered that the high biodiversity of tree frogs at Amazonian sites is related to the fact that different groups of them have lived alongside each other in the Amazon basin for more than 60 million years.

Because palms inhabit tropical rainforests, and are often found in remote locations that are difficult to access, species that are new to science are still being discovered. In 2009 alone, the year after the second edition of *Genera Palmarum* was published, twenty-four new species of palm were identified, twenty of which came from Madagascar. And at Kew, Baker has just published fifteen new species of *Calamus*, the main rattan genus, and is currently naming another three new single-species genera, including one that will bear Alfred Russel Wallace's name. Some of the new species are incredibly rare; for example, fewer than ten individuals of one species, the stemless palm *Dypsis humilis*, were found in north-east Madagascar and it is not known whether other populations exist elsewhere. They were growing within a patch of forest used heavily by local people for timber, so the likelihood of the palm becoming extinct, before scientists have even had a chance to study it in detail, is very high.

Palms are highly useful plants. They provide us with numerous products – oils, drinks, coconuts, dates, rattan, fibres and thatching materials – many of which help to sustain rural populations across the tropics. With many rainforest ecosystems facing pressures from logging, clearance for agriculture and climate change, botanists are engaged in a race against time to find and record new palm species. For *Tahina spectabilis*, of which only a handful of wild plants are known to exist, the story is a relatively happy one; seeds from the palm have now been propagated and are being distributed,

African oil palm plantation in Cameroon

in Madagascar and across the world, in the hope of increasing the plant's numbers. Revenues from seed sales go back to the local community so that they can benefit from their precious palm.

For the palms that have yet to be found and classified, the story is less optimistic. Sometimes the process of assembling the evidence to formally describe a new plant species in a credible journal can take months or even years. 'We must find quicker and more expedient ways of getting biodiversity information out there,' urges Baker. 'For as long as a species is not described, it doesn't exist in the eyes of policy-makers or the IUCN [International Union for Conservation of Nature] Red List of threatened species, so it can't be conserved.' And if, as Kew's work suggests, palm diversity has built up over 100 million years, it will require that long to rebuild it, if its rainforest habitats are destroyed by humans.

23

CAPTURE AND
DRAW-DOWN

Collecting *Cinchona* bark in San Juan Valley, Peru,
in the nineteenth century

As far back as the middle of the nineteenth century, the botanist Richard Spruce realised that human activity was not treating the world's flora and fauna kindly. During the fifteen years of collecting trips he made to South America he deduced that if humans wished to put plants to use, they would have to conserve them: 'Whilst the demand for such precious substances as Peruvian bark, sarsparilla, caoutchouc, &c. must necessarily go on increasing, the supply yielded by the forest will decrease, and ultimately fail,' he wrote.

George Perkins Marsh, who is now considered to be the father of the American Conservation Movement, challenged the general belief that humanity's effect on the natural world was a positive one in 1864 in *Man and Nature*, arguing that the ancient civilisations around the Mediterranean had brought about their own collapse by deforesting their hillsides and thus eroding their soil. Parks such as Yosemite and Yellowstone were subsequently established in America to preserve areas of wilderness. But it was not until after the Second World War that concern over human impacts on the environment became global.

The first list of plants under threat, produced in 1970, suggested that 20,000 plant species needed some form of protection to survive.

Then, in 1992, the United Nations Conference on Environment and Development, the first international Earth Summit, gave rise to the Convention on Biological Diversity and calls to protect endangered species and environments. A new word entered the political discourse: 'biodiversity'. This was defined as 'variability among living organisms from all sources including, inter alia, terrestrial, marine and other aquatic ecosystems along with ecological complexes of which they are part; this includes diversity within species, between species and of ecosystems.'

For the following twenty years, attention focused on identifying areas with the highest concentration of biodiversity hotspots and threatened species. Many global initiatives targeted these areas. Now 13 per cent of the earth's terrestrial regions are protected, and the International Union for Conservation of Nature (IUCN) regularly publishes 'Red Lists' of threatened species to help highlight ones that are approaching extinction.

Despite these efforts, however, governments have failed to deliver the target set by the Convention on Biological Diversity in 2002 – to achieve, by 2010, a significant reduction of the current rate of biodiversity loss at global, regional and national levels. Biodiversity loss has, in most cases, continued unabated.

There is a plethora of reasons why this target has been missed and many politicians and policymakers ask 'so what?'. With global challenges such as climate change, population growth, fuel security and urbanisation placing ever greater demands on land, they question whether biodiversity has become a luxury we can no longer afford.

In 2005 a landmark study was published that changed the political landscape for conservation, probably for ever. Rather than viewing biodiversity as something to be conserved for conservation's sake, the Millennium Ecosystem Assessment started to assess the contributions that biodiversity and biodiverse ecosystems made to human livelihoods and well-being. For the first time, biodiversity was viewed as a commodity and assessed according to its contributions to humanity. These include provisioning services (the biodiversity that provides food, fresh water, wood, fibre and fuel); regulating services (modulate climate, floods and diseases, as well as purifying water); and cultural services (which confer aesthetic, spiritual, educational and recreational benefits).

This represents a fairly radical departure from the previously followed model, where the areas containing the highest concentrations of species or threatened species were conserved. Imagine a landscape including a stand of forest, fields, trees around the field-margins and a backdrop of mountains covered with sparse vegetation. Under traditional 'protected area' strategies, you would probably aim to enclose and protect the forest, on the basis that this almost certainly represents the most species-rich area in the landscape. In contrast, within an ecosystem service assessment, the forest represents an important resource for carbon draw-down (the process by which plants remove carbon dioxide from the atmosphere during photosynthesis) and prevention of soil erosion (regulating services), while the trees around the edge of the fields offer significant foraging and nesting habitats for pollinators (regulating service), the fields themselves are important for growing crops (provisioning service) and the mountains host the water sources of rivers that irrigate crops, and are of recreational and possibly spiritual significance (cultural services). The landscape therefore becomes partitioned in a very different way. Such an approach requires scientists to identify the ecosystem services provided by the biodiversity, then to calculate their value to society and the costs involved in maintaining them.

This 'new' approach has been widely accepted by governments.

In 2012 the Intergovernmental Platform on Biodiversity and Ecosystem Services was established to assess the state of the planet's biodiversity, its ecosystems and the essential services they provide to society. But the question of which services are essential to society is, as yet, unanswered. The United Nations Environment Programme recently proposed that nations should aim for a 'Green Economy'. It defined this as 'one that results in improved human well-being and social equity, while significantly reducing environmental risks and ecological scarcities'. Importantly it suggested that biodiversity would be needed to achieve this.

One of the biggest environmental risks facing humankind today is climate change. This phenomenon is being driven by the increasing concentration of carbon dioxide in the atmosphere, which has now reached 400 ppm (parts per million). Put into context, this is approximately 120 ppm more than at any other time in the past 800,000 years (the period over which we have obtained good records of atmospheric carbon dioxide from ice-core records).

We urgently need to find ways to reduce the amount of carbon dioxide in the atmosphere, and in this regard plants are vital. Trees are among the organisms that are most effective at removing carbon dioxide from the atmosphere – which they do as part of photosynthesis with carbon becoming sequestered in their wood, leaves and roots. The essential role of plants in regulating the atmosphere has been known for a long time, but it is only in the past few decades that the importance of trees has become properly realised. Trees provide an important carbon dioxide 'sink' that currently accounts for almost all of the carbon extracted from the atmosphere by the biosphere (the area of earth where organisms live, including the ground and air). Tree species that grow quickly are common, end up large and live for a long time are the biggest immediate carbon sinks. There are many examples, but in the tropics the

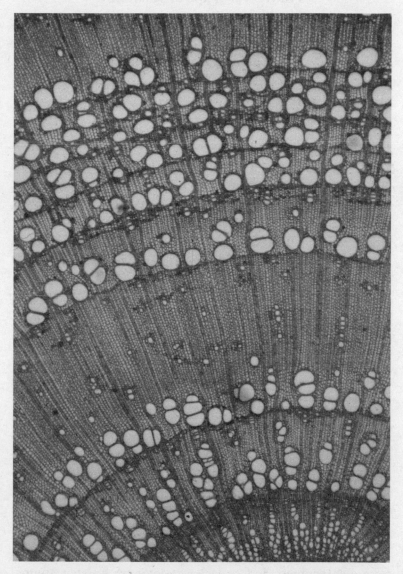
Tree rings seen at microscopic level. Trees are highly efficient at taking up carbon dioxide, with carbon becoming captured in the wood, leaves and roots

Brazil nut tree of the Amazon rainforest (*Bertholletia excelsa*), Africa's red ironwood (*Lophira alata*) and various common and large hardwood trees in Asia are important when it comes to drawing down carbon dioxide. In temperate regions, giants such as California redwoods and *Fitzroya* in Chile are probably very important because they are fast growing but grow to huge size and persist for centuries.

Estimates suggest that in the years 2000–2007 the global forest carbon sink extracted 2.5 billion tonnes of carbon from the atmosphere each year. Globally, the tropical forests absorb the most atmospheric carbon dioxide at 1.3 billion tonnes a year, followed by temperate forests (at 0.78 billion tonnes) and boreal forests (0.5 billion tonnes). Interestingly, however, regrowth tropical forests – tropical forests that are recovering from past deforestation and logging that exhibit relatively rapid early forest growth – provide the largest sink, accounting for up to 1.7 billion tonnes of carbon a year. The younger, faster growing trees take up a lot more carbon than mature, slower growing trees.

In a sense this is a 'good news' story – all is not lost and once land is abandoned and tropical forest starts to recover, it will immediately start work drawing down atmospheric carbon dioxide. This is certainly a line of thought currently used by carbon traders who see these areas as an important investment opportunity: buy up degraded forest and in thirty years' time it will be forest again, drawing down atmospheric carbon dioxide that can then be used both in trading and in carbon offsets.

But recent work conducted at Kew offers a note of caution. Kew scientist Lydia Cole examined the rate of recovery of tropical forest following disturbances by looking at fossil pollen sequences from sites spanning the four major areas: South America, Central America, Africa and South-East Asia. She examined the time taken for the forests to recover and found huge variations. Some areas

Tropical forest in Singapore

recovered quickly and had returned to forest within thirty years. However, other regions took up to 500 years to become wooded once more. The average rate of tropical forest recovery was 250 years. There were also some remarkable differences between regions. Forests in Central America recovered the quickest, those in South America the slowest. The type of disturbance also affected recovery rates: forests returned much more rapidly to their original state after natural disasters such as hurricanes and fires than they did after human disturbances. More work is needed to explain what this variability tells us.

As for the trees that decorate our urban landscapes, they too offer potential to influence the carbon 'budget'. A recent study estimated the total storage of carbon by trees in US urban areas to be approximately 643 million tonnes. These trees absorbed approximately 25.6 million tonnes of atmospheric carbon a year, about 1 per cent of the global total. It is a small, but significant contribution, encouraging to the city-dwellers who gaze at the trees out of their office windows, sit beneath them with their lunchtime sandwiches and breathe the air they help to regulate.

So how good are Kew Gardens' 14,000 trees at sucking carbon dioxide out of London's air? Using similar methods to those employed in the US study, Kew taxonomist Tim Harris has determined that even in this small corner of West London, the trees draw down up to 8.6 tonnes of carbon dioxide per year.

The risk represented by increasing levels of atmospheric carbon dioxide is a global issue. Understanding what to protect, where and when is likely to have huge ramifications. At the same time, there is the need to mitigate the risks to humanity associated with scarce plants and animals.

Take bees. Throughout Europe and the USA there has been a dramatic decline in bee numbers over the past decade, and this

Trees in Kew Gardens are estimated to draw down 8.6 tonnes of
carbon dioxide a year

has resulted in an associated reduction in pollination, an ecosystem
service. The reasons behind this decline are complex and, as yet,
poorly understood. However, a study of biodiversity at the
molecular level has provided intriguing insights, which could help
solve the problem.

As it happens, coffee could be part of the solution. Caffeine is
used by plants as a defence against herbivorous insects.
Unsurprisingly, it can be found playing this role in the bitter-
tasting beans of coffee and in the young leaves of tea. But, as Kew
scientist Phil Stevenson and his colleagues discovered, caffeine also
occurs in the nectar of the flowers of the coffee plant. Nectar, of
course, is the reward with which flowers tempt their natural pollinators to come inside, so the nectar of the coffee plant only
contains caffeine at concentrations that are below the bees' taste

threshold, and therefore has no repellent effect. Instead, results from Stevenson's team demonstrate that caffeine improves bee memory for flower cues associated with the food reward of nectar. It was already well known that floral characteristics such as odour, colour and shape are critical in enabling bees to recognise and remember flowers as good food choices. It seems that eating caffeine-infused nectar will cause the bees to remember the particular set of cues from that plant better than those conveyed by other plants, and will therefore be visited more often, leading to better and more frequent pollination. It's a fascinating insight into how plants gain a competitive edge over other species.

Work is now under way to exploit the memory-enhancing effect of caffeine by using it to train commercial bees, which farmers buy to improve pollination in soft fruits. Strawberries require several pollination events over several days to ensure the fruit quality and yields to meet the standards demanded by consumers in the UK. Wild pollinators are in decline and do not provide an adequate pollination service, so farmers go to considerable expense to intro-duce colonies of bumblebees to augment pollination and ensure they obtain a bumper crop. However, these commercial bees are distracted by hedgerow plant species, which reduce their efficiency for pollinating strawberries. Kew scientists are therefore training the commercial bees *in situ* to improve their forage focus on strawberry flowers by using a mixture of slow-release strawberry odour derived from the flowers and supplementary nest diets containing caffeine. The bees will remember the strawberries better than other species, leading to better pollination, better yields, reduced costs to farmers and lesser impacts on wild species and their natural pollinators.

We all know you can roast, boil up and drink the little brown seed of the fragrant, sweet Arabica coffee (*Coffea arabica*). And now we know you can also use it to help bees recognise strawberry plants. This example represents just a tiny fraction of the untapped potential of biodiversity, zooming from forests down to molecular compounds in providing regulating services and reducing environment risk. The potential is huge, yet most of it is still unrealised and unvalued. Tapping into this potential and calculating its monetary worth will help us all realise how important plants are to our lives.

24

GREEN AND PLEASANT LANDS

Cascade waterfall at Hestercombe Gardens, designed by
Copleston Warre Bampfyde in the 1750s

A s IDEAS CHANGE, words change with them. Green used to be a colour. Now it's a lifestyle, a philosophy, a political aspiration. Our government wants to be 'the greenest on record' (which would have puzzled earlier generations of politicians, for whom a 'green' was something on a golf course, not a candidate in an election). At international level, the United Nations has produced its framework for the 'Green Economy', a phrase which would have meant nothing just a few decades ago.

Our relationship with Nature has become an integral part of how humans conduct politics, build our houses, teach our children and run our economies. As we have seen in Chapter 23, gaining what we want from that relationship requires a way of measuring the value we get from it. Nature provides us with services, which, like any other, we need to quantify, evaluate and factor into our plans for our world. This is a new idea, and it has new terms to go with it: 'natural capital'; 'ecosystem services'. Some of the most important services that are now being recognised are those that underpin human well-being. As well as helping to regulate our planet, biodiversity provides aesthetic, spiritual, educational and recreational services.

City-dwellers, in particular, need their parks and trees. London has always been good at this. Its constructed environment might make it, in the words of author Peter Ackroyd, one of its keenest observers, 'an ugly city', but its parks are one of the urban glories of Europe.

These parks, along with playgrounds and back gardens, are in effect islands of biodiversity that provide food and shelter for all sorts of wildlife. But these green spaces aren't important just for our wildlife; we are not conserving biodiversity purely for its own sake, we are conserving places of recreation and leisure for ourselves. They provide an important resource for humanity: an ecosystem service. They have value: natural capital.

Kew provides this in spades. It's also, of course, a place of serious science. But the two have not always lived happily in harmony.

In the nineteenth century, the artistic movement of Romanticism drew on Nature as a source of inspiration. Painters such as Constable and Turner captured the landscape in all its majesty, poets such as Wordsworth and Coleridge built a whole natural philosophy from striding through the Lake District, and composers such as Mendelssohn and Beethoven evoked storms and seascapes as a vehicle for profound psychological insights. Few went as far as the American author Henry David Thoreau, who spent two years, two months and two days living in a log cabin on the shores of a lake in Massachusetts: 'I went to the woods because I wished to live deliberately, to front only the essential facts of life, and see if I could not learn what it had to teach, and not, when I came to die, discover that I had not lived.' He wrote up the experience in exhaustive detail in his 1854 book *Walden* and has remained the hero of back-to-Nature types ever since.

Serious scientists such as Joseph Hooker, as Director of Kew, had no time for this sort of stuff, and still less for the idea that his botanical garden should be a place of genteel relaxation for the general public. Kew's 'primary objects', thundered Hooker, 'are scientific and utilitarian, not recreational'. This was no place for 'mere pleasure or recreation seekers . . . whose motives are rude romping and games'. They could do their romping and admire their ghastly municipal planting in their local park, not at Kew. Hooker insisted that nobody except serious botanical students and artists should be allowed into the Gardens before lunch, and fiercely resisted all attempts to extend the hours the gardens were open to the general public.

More democratic spirits took an opposite view, including the MP Acton Smee Ayrton, Commissioner at the Office of Works which took over control of Kew from the Woods and Forests Department in 1850. Ayrton saw the burgeoning interest in botany and gardening among the general public as a good thing. For women, in particular, it provided an arena for their interest and passion at a time when the world of science was almost entirely a male preserve. War broke out over the begonias between Hooker and his opponents. When things got personal, Hooker's notorious cantankerousness didn't help: even his supporter and friend Darwin described him as 'impulsive and somewhat peppery in temper'. There was also a fierce rivalry between Kew and the British Museum's natural history department (later to become the Natural History Museum), with each claiming important botanical collections. Things came to a head when Ayrton sided with Richard Owen of the Natural History Museum. Their idea of moving Kew's precious Herbarium to South Kensington would have left it as little more than a public park. But Hooker (backed by Darwin and geologist Charles Lyell) won the day. Following debates in both Houses of Parliament, the Gardens retained their vital collections and Ayrton was eventually removed from his position overseeing Kew. When he went on to lose his seat at the next election, it no doubt gave Hooker a certain amount of satisfaction.

NOTICE

IS HEREBY GIVEN,

THAT BY THE

GRACIOUS PERMISSION OF HER MAJESTY,

THE

ROYAL
PLEASURE GROUNDS
AT KEW

Will be opened to the Public on every Day in the Week from the 18th of May, until Tuesday, the 30th of September, during the present Year,—on Sundays, from 2 o'clock P.M., and on every other Day in the Week from 1 o'clock P.M.

THE ACCESS to these Grounds will be in the Kew and Richmond Road, by the "Lion" and "Unicorn" Gates respectively; and, on the River Side of the Grounds by the Gate adjoining to the Brentford Ferry; the Entrance Gates to the Botanic Gardens on Kew Green being open as heretofore.

Communications will be opened between the Botanic Gardens and the Pleasure Gardens by Gates in the Wire Fence which separates the two.

It is requested that Visitors will abstain from carrying Baskets, Parcels, or Refreshments of any kind into the Grounds. Smoking in the Botanic Gardens is strictly prohibited. No Dogs admitted.

By Order of the Right Honourable the First Commissioner of Her Majesty's Works, &c.

Office of Works, April 15, 1856.

PRINTED BY HARRISON AND SONS, ST. MARTIN'S LANE.

Poster announcing opening times for Kew Gardens, 1856

Hooker may have won the battle, but he didn't win the war. The end result was that Kew remained as a centre of scientific excellence, not instead of providing a place for the public to enjoy, but as well as. Today's scientists know that it can, and must, do both, and that both are equally important to human society and well-being. And, crucially, to human health.

As explained in Chapter 1, some of the earliest versions of the botanical garden were the medieval 'physic' gardens, growing herbs and plants for medicinal purposes. From the sixteenth century, physic gardens sprang up to provide pharmaceutical plants for university medical schools at places like Pisa and Padua in Italy, and Montpellier in France. Gardens were places of study, too: in ancient Greece people would gather to debate and learn under a grove of olive trees, the origin of the phrase the 'Groves of Academe'.

Many of the early pioneering gardener-medics were monks and other religious men, working, exercising and praying in the monastery garden. Now as then, the garden is a supplier of resources such as food and medicines, and a provider of relaxation and contemplation: it has natural capital and provides ecosystem services.

This link between the preservation of natural sites and religion is, and always has been, significant. Mesopotamian and Egyptian temples had gardens. Sacred groves spread across India as Hindu 'living temples'. Buddhist gardens flourished in China and Japan. Shinto shrines were often built with sacred gardens, where the Japanese cedar received particular veneration. Norsemen had groves where every tree was sacred, and ritual human sacrifice took place beneath the branches. In the monasteries and convents of Medieval Europe 'Mary gardens', filled with flowers, plants and trees symbolic of the Virgin Mary, were designed to bring the visitor closer to God, just as the Bible says the Garden of Gethsemane did the three Marys on Easter Day.

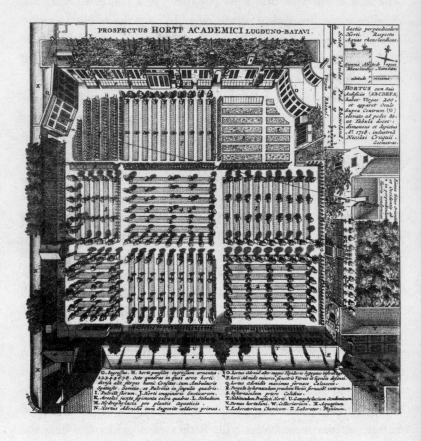

Plan of Leiden Botanical Garden, 1720

'There are still many pagan sacred spaces, not just in Britain but across the world', says Shonil Bhagwat, Lecturer in Geography at the Open University, whose research includes links between conservation and sacred land. 'They are normally stone circles or henges, but these are often associated with old-growth vegetation. Also in Britain there are thousands of old yew trees that have been surveyed and written about.' There's no mistaking the spiritual significance of these grand old men of so many of England's ancient parish churchyards, their branches spreading benevolently over centuries' worth of village graves. Author Thomas Hardy got to the heart of their place in the turning cycle of human life: 'Portion of this yew is a man my grand-sire knew . . .'

'Sacred spaces take very different shapes and forms,' says Bhagwat. One study found natural sacred sites in temple groves, indigenous forests, sections within agro-forestry projects, on the banks of sacred rivers, along coastlines and beside sacred lakes. This variety and wide geographical spread make sacred sites an ideal resource for preserved biodiversity.

India is a good example. The country's Centre for Science and Environment records around 14,000 sacred groves in India today. Their status and protection by local communities has preserved them against logging and other destructive activities, making them precious reservoirs of biodiversity, from scrub forests in Rajasthan to rainforests in Kerala. In one sacred grove in the Meghalaya region, half the plant species have been classified as rare by local botanists, including some that had been thought for decades to have vanished from the area.

Some of these groves are now the only local source of traditional medicinal plants such as the *nataknar* tree (used to treat stomach disorders in precious local cattle) or *gometi* (*Melothria heterophylla*), an edible mulberry. Other Indian groves are a source of plants such as the flowering shrub *Carissa carandas*, the roots and flowers of which are used to treat scabies and fever and stomach disorders. Indian sacred groves also serve as community kitchen gardens. Villagers in Western India head to groves for concentrations of plants such as the *chirpal* tree (*Zanthoxylum rhetsa*) for their berries, as well as dried flowers used to spice local dishes. Groves in Konkan, meanwhile, are foraged for small edible mushrooms known as *chitlea*.

In the region of Maharashtra, villagers have begun documenting the biodiversity in their local sacred groves with a specific practical purpose. 'A lot of people keep coming here. They all seem to be interested in the trees and plants that grow in the grove. This used to intrigue us. What is it that attracts so many educated people?' says Dharma Lokande, a local primary school teacher. 'So we started keeping records of the local trees and plants. Our ultimate aim is to prevent outsiders, especially pharmaceutical companies, from taking advantage of our ignorance.'

Some sacred sites represent havens for rare natural habitats. In Japan the sacred grove at Shimogamo contains around 40 species of deciduous trees including zelkova and hackberry up to 600 years old, the only place where the original wilderness of the southern Kyoto prefecture remains. The sacred grove at Yahiko in Niigata prefecture features a *chinquapin* tree enshrined in its own holy precinct. Other sacred groves in Japan such as Seifa on Okinawa provide havens for indigenous trees like *kubanoki* (a kind of palm) and *yabunikkei* (*Cinnamomum yabunikkei*), a form of wild cinnamon. A forest of nagi (a variety of *Podocarpus*) beckons at the Kasuga sacred grove in Nara, alongside 100 other species of tree and shrub including kasuga cedar, ichii oak and andromeda, which earned the area UNESCO World Heritage Site status in 1998.

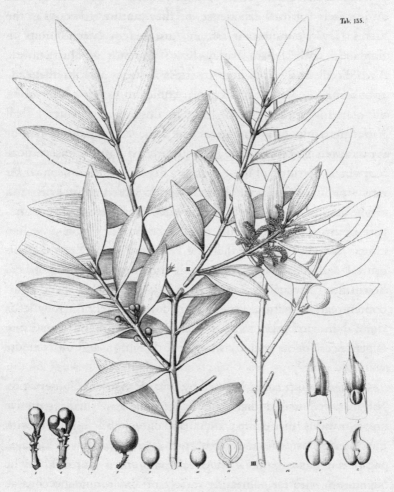

Tab. 135.

PODOCARPUS Nageia.

Podocarpus, the Nagi tree

Areas of diversity can be 'spiritually' enriching whether or not you follow a religion. 'There are many stands of trees that provide an intensely spiritual experience, be they mature redwoods in the Sierra Nevada, mountain ash in Australia or beech forests in England,' says Richard Barley, Kew's Director of Horticulture. And Shonil Bhagwat is keen to stress linkages and interdependence across all such sites: 'When it comes to nature conservation on a highly anthropogenic [human dominated] planet it's all about networks of green spaces,' he says. 'An individual tree or grove might be perceived as insignificant for nature conservation, but when you think of these sites as a network it becomes a whole new way of looking at the natural world. Sacred natural sites and territories can be considered on the earth as a network of acupuncture points would be on the human body. They have a healing effect. We also consider that the relationship between them is critical and they cannot be seen in isolation from each other.' Scientifically valuable biodiversity walks hand in hand with contemplation: natural capital and ecosystem service. Kew leads the way in combining its scientific work with providing uplifting experiences for its many visitors from London and all over the world.

A recent report commissioned by Botanic Gardens Conservation International mused that 'botanic gardens have made tentative steps towards broadening their audiences and engaging with community concerns and needs', but argued that few of Britain's 130-plus botanic gardens were achieving their potential to be 'significant sites for addressing social and environmental changes that will concern us all'. The report wants people to understand plants as well as enjoy them: 'I am constantly aware of the need to plan and deliver a rich and stimulating blend of sensory experiences, while ensuring that the underpinning value and integrity of our living collections is also strengthened,' says Richard Barley. The report proposes: 'In a society where many people have become disconnected from the natural world but where the threats from climate change and species extinction are predicted to get worse as the century progresses, botanic gardens could play an important role in reconnecting people with the world of plants.'

An example of one project that is successfully engaging visitors is the 'Shelf Life' project at Chelsea Physic Garden. Plants grow through the packaging of familiar products that are made from them: wheat sprouts in a biscuit tin, potatoes from crisp packets, peanuts through a peanut butter jar. Visitors love it. Children are amazed to discover which plants are in which food products. It's an antidote to the (probably apocryphal) story of the schoolchild who was asked to draw a chicken, and drew one wrapped in clingfilm, with a Tesco label stuck to its breast.

As Barley confirms: 'Most botanic gardens are doing interesting things to provide visitors with a diverse range of experiences . . . bold visual design, aromatic gardens, incorporation of sound-generating elements, children's landscapes and so forth. There is an increased awareness of the need to ensure that the visitor's experience is memorable, engaging and perhaps transforming.'

Barley is a fan of guerilla gardening, where green-fingered activists 'take over' unlovely or derelict spaces and transform them with plants. 'Fantastic', he says, simply. 'What a superb realisation of the potential benefit of public will and spontaneous opportunity.'

There are many kinds of green space. Preserving their biodiversity is certainly good for the planet, but it's also good for us.

25

THE GREAT PROVIDERS

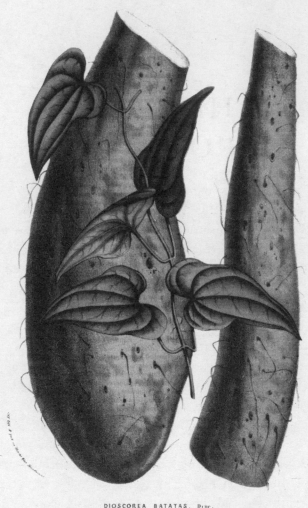

DIOSCOREA BATATAS. Dene.
Igname de Chine. (Rhizôme de grand nat.)

The yam has much to offer as a 'new' food crop

WHEN KEW WAS in its infancy in the late eighteenth century, with Joseph Banks at the helm, the outlook for Britain was optimistic. Empire and industry were opening up new opportunities in the West for transport and trade. Although hunger was still an issue for many, medical advances and greater wealth were making people healthier, so the birth rate was rising. And the world's diverse flora was revealing itself to contain a glut of species with potential in the fields of science or enterprise. As Chapter 2 explained, Banks's vision was to use this emerging botanical resource to make the so-called 'wastelands' of the world productive, in order to feed Britain's growing population while contributing to the continued success of the Empire.

Although Banks was not able to fully realise his goal, his successors at Kew founded botanical gardens around the world that helped develop lucrative, plant-based commodities. Coffee, oranges, almonds, rubber and mahogany were just a few of the plants grown, with the aid of Kew, in Britain's colonies. Joseph Chamberlain acknowledged this formally in the House of Commons in 1898 when he was Colonial Secretary, saying: 'I do not think it is too much to say that at the present time there are several of our important Colonies which owe whatever prosperity they possess to the knowledge and experience of, and the assistance given by, the authorities at Kew Gardens.'

The colonial era did not deliver all it promised. When the British Empire disintegrated, independent nations struggled to overcome its legacy. The introduction of industrialisation had changed the world's climate in ways that we are only now beginning to understand. Natural ecosystems had been altered in favour of carving out agricultural landscapes and building cities, injuring the vital ecosystem services required to keep the earth habitable. With our global population expected to rise from its current level of 7.1 billion to 9.7 billion by 2050, and with limited additional land resources available for farming, feeding the world will present a considerable challenge in future.

Despite this uneasy legacy, there are elements of Banks's vision that we can draw on in our efforts to reverse some of the more recent damage inflicted on our planet. For a start, whatever methods we use to help resolve the current, most critical issues, they need to be worldwide in their ambition, as climate change, biodiversity loss and pollution do not respect national boundaries. And, just as Banks saw plants as potentially valuable commodities, we need to understand the economic value of the world's biodiversity. With today's economic model based on ever-increasing production and consumption, it is imperative that we uncouple fiscal growth from environmental damage. This means placing a sufficiently high value on ecosystems and the services they provide, so that governments and businesses appreciate their economic value to society and their contribution to human well-being. If we don't conserve biodiversity, we run the risk of losing the vital ecosystem services that it provides. And, as hindsight has shown us, replacing these with alternative, artificial, services, often turns out to be much more costly and to have even greater impact on some of the world's poorest people.

Having been at the centre of plant science for two and a half centuries, Kew is ideally placed to contribute to resolving the world-wide challenges of climate and land-use change, as well as debates and initiatives related to increasing sustainability. The unrivalled collections of specimens in its Millennium Seed Bank, Herbarium and Fungarium – together with the taxonomists, systematists and geneticists who work within them – represent an extraordinary global resource for understanding the role that plants and fungi contribute to humanity. Kew's 300-plus plant scientists and technicians have in-depth knowledge of the world's flora, including species that repre-sent potential new foods, biofuels and commodities. And, perhaps most importantly, Kew has a growing store of genetic material within the plant tissues of its live collections that can help in a practical way to redress the impacts of biodiversity loss and climate change, by breeding genetic variability and resilience back into modern crops.

Sixty per cent of our food energy intake comes from just three edible plants, rice, maize and wheat (*above*)

PricewaterhouseCoopers (PwC) undertook a study to calculate the monetary value of the genetically diverse plants that are the wild relatives of modern-day crops. As Chapter 14 explained, these crop wild relatives (CWRs) contain useful traits such as drought tolerance and resilience to climatic variation. Such traits have been bred out of many modern crops in favour of genes that give higher yields and better flavour. However, if crops are to cope with the climate changes that we can expect in the future, they need to be able to adapt to variable weather. The only solution is to find the genetically diverse crop wild relatives of modern crops and use them to ensure that the desired traits are bred back into modern agricultural cultivars. PwC concluded that the genetic wild relatives of today's agricultural crops were worth US $200 billion (£116 billion) to the world's agricultural industry.

Richard Thompson, one of the partners, explains how the figure was reached:

We analysed lots of data, we talked to about forty people in the industry and we gathered as much information as we could to demonstrate the yield improvement from using CWRs. Then we translated that into a big financial model, which said, 'The impact on the yield is X.' We built up a set of assumptions to try to identify what proportion of the observed yield improvements was due to the use of CWR traits within the crop. Then we converted that into dollars in terms of the benefit to production at the factory gate. We looked at three crops to begin with: wheat, rice and potatoes. We picked those because they are grown globally and there was a fair amount of research already on the impact CWRs have had on them. We then extrapolated our results across all crops that use CWRs, which gave us the total benefit of US $200 billion.

Although this may seem a huge value, it is supported by good evidence that using CWRs has a considerable benefit in increasing yields. Take potato blight, for example, the disease that devastated Irish farming in the mid-nineteenth century. One of the reasons the blight was so damaging was that farmers at that time were universally using a variety called 'Lumper'. This was propagated vegetatively, which meant that all the potatoes were genetically identical clones. Worse still, 'Lumper' was particularly susceptible to the *Phytophthora infestans* stramenopile that caused the disease. Adding genetic diversity to modern potato varieties is one method used by farmers today to avoid a repetition of this problem.

'There are lots of studies that show using CWRs reduces the impact of potato blight by up to 30 per cent,' says Richard. 'In other words, you get a 30 per cent benefit in yield on potatoes through using certain CWRs. When you look at that across the whole supply chain, the value to the industry can be substantial.'

Other studies have been set up to evaluate the benefits to individual farmers of the ecosystem services provided by biodiversity, including pollination. It is widely appreciated that insect pollination (particularly by bees) is needed for many plants to reproduce, from apples and onions to kale. What is less well known is that without the appropriate landscape features, including suitable nesting habitats close enough to the crops, pollination is severely diminished. This is because most bee species can't fly much further than 1 kilometre before needing to feed. So if we reduce the numbers of biodiverse patches that provide such habitats, near to fields of crops, it can have a significant impact.

This point was neatly demonstrated in a project undertaken jointly by researchers from the World Wildlife Fund, Stanford University and the University of Kansas in the USA. They sought to illustrate the potential economic value of conserving biodiverse forest patches within agricultural landscapes. The scientists examined the data on farm yields and market prices, in order to estimate the monetary worth that could be placed on pollination by wild bees living in patches of tropical forest adjacent to a single coffee farm in Costa Rica.

They found that the distance from these biodiverse forest patches (which provided important nesting habitats for bees) directly influenced the coffee produced, with yields higher by 20 per cent in areas of the farm lying within approximately 1 kilometre of the forest. By reducing the frequency of 'peaberries' (which occur when only partial fertilisation takes place, with just one of the two coffee seeds in each coffee cherry being fertilised, resulting in a smaller bean), pollination also improved coffee quality near wooded parts by 27 per cent. The researchers calculated that pollination by bees from the forest patches equated to around US $60,000 (£35,000) in income for the year 2002 to 2003. Conserving such patches increases biodiversity as well as sustaining ecosystem services. Calculating the financial benefits of similar services, such as carbon storage and water purification, would help create a solid case for paying landowners to conserve forest fragments within agricultural and other inhabited areas.

The coffee industry is particularly vulnerable to biodiversity loss and climate change. Coffee is an unusual commodity in that, although there are 124 known species, only two are used for major commercial production of coffee. These are *Coffea arabica* (Arabica) and *C. canephora (robusta)*. Of these, *C. arabica* produces the best-tasting coffee and is the species used within the speciality industry. It probably originated in Ethiopia, formed when *C. canephora* and *C. eugenioides* hybridised, in a one-off event, some 50,000–1 million years ago. *Coffea arabica* started to be distributed in the fifteenth century and, as farmers started growing it on

Tab. 130.

COFFEA ARABICA L.

Der Arabische Caffee.

The coffee plant, *Coffea arabica*

plantations that were often established from a single plant, its genetic diversity dwindled. 'In all the plantations around the world there is probably less than 1 per cent of the genetic variation you can find today in Ethiopia,' says Aaron Davis, Head of Coffee Research in Kew's Herbarium.

Those plants today constitute the world's second most valuable international commodity. Although genetic traits such as resilience to disease or drought can be bred back into genetically poor cultivars, time could be running out for *C. arabica*. A study carried out by Kew in 2012 found that, by 2080, climate change could have reduced the suitable environments for the existence of wild *C. arabica* in Ethiopia and South Sudan by between 65 and 100 per cent. This has important implications for the future of the industry. Coffee supports the livelihoods of 25 million farming families worldwide, more than 100 million people. 'The environment will not be the same in 2080 as it is now,' explains Justin Moat of Kew's Geographic Information Systems Unit, who was involved with modelling future climate scenarios for the study. 'We now know what the climatic conditions then might be, so we can say, "If we're going to grow coffee, we can do so here or we can move it there." Something can be done about it; we have the information and we have the time, too.'

But, as importantly, if *C. arabica* ultimately fails, it is reassuring to know that we can try some of the presently unexploited coffee species, although, worryingly, many of these are also located in habitats that are threatened, particularly from land-use change. Sixty-one species of coffee, for example, grow in Madagascar. It is possible that non-commercial coffee species could yield other benefits too. The nineteenth-century explorer, David Livingstone, reported seeing coffee wood being used to make huts in sub-Saharan Africa. It has potential for furniture making, since it provides a straight, dense, strong timber that is partially resistant to termites. Its fruits and leaves are also used as a food (with green beans used as diet agents), its leaves to make tea, and other beverages are made from juice of the fleshy parts of the fruit.

In terms of 'new' food crops, the yam (*Dioscorea* species) has much to offer. Six hundred species of yam grow in the tropics, ranging from wild endemics (species unique to that area) to highly valuable, cultivated varieties. Yams are a major food source in tropical and subtropical regions, especially in West Africa, but tend to be overlooked in favour of grain crops where those are available. Nonetheless, they are an important back-up for when other crops fail. 'They are a famine food,' explains Paul Wilkin, a yam expert within Kew's Herbarium. 'When times get tough, people eat yams.'

With the impending global challenges of climate change and population rise, which are particularly acute in Africa and Asia, yams may well prove to be useful alternatives to current crops. As tubers, they have large underground storage reservoirs, which make them robust and well suited to drier climates. Cereals, such as maize and rice, require significant amounts of water and often fail when drought strikes. As Wilkin explains, 'Yams are a good, safe way forward and scientists could look at ways of breeding them to make them more amenable to conventional agriculture. At the moment they are what we call an orphan crop: one that doesn't get the full attention of the world's financial systems. They might not be everyone's preferred food but they are definitely a good bet for ensuring everyone has something to eat.'

The examples of coffee and yams demonstrate just how important Kew's plant intelligence is for identifying potential new commodities: in effect, continuing one of the key roles for Kew that was originally identified by its Georgian and Victorian custodians. If Joseph Banks returned to Kew today, he would surely approve of the Gardens' objective of using its unrivalled expertise, gained over 250 years, to help underpin resilient food and drink supplies for future generations. Being strongly motivated to make the most of plants' potential as commodities, he would no doubt be happy, too, to hear of Kew's past role in shaping industries such as rubber. (Hopefully he would also take some responsibility for the devastating impact that these colonial enterprises have had on human welfare and the intricately connected world of plants.)

The legacy that might surprise Banks the most, though, is that the African cycad and food plant *Encephalartos altensteinii*, brought back by the first plant hunter he despatched overseas, is still going strong in the Palm House. Like Kew itself, it has been at the heart of the many changes botanical science has undergone since blossoming in the eighteenth century, and it is set to thrive for many years to come.

ACKNOWLEDGEMENTS

The authors would like to thank the following people for their helpful advice and edits during the writing of this book: Bill Baker, Richard Barley, Henk Beentje, Paul Cannon, Mark Chase, Colin Clubbe, Aaron Davis, Steve Davis, Iain Darbyshire, Bryn Dentinger, John Dransfield, Lauren Gardiner, Tim Harris, Andrew Jackson, Tony Kirkham, Geoffrey Kite, Ilia Leitch, Viswambharan Sarasan, André Schuiteman, Monique Simmonds, Nigel Veitch, Lucy Smith, Paul Smith, Wolfgang Stuppy, Scott Taylor, Oliver Whaley and Paul Wilkin of the Royal Botanic Gardens, Kew; Linda Brooks and Gina Douglas of the Linnean Society of London; and Shonil Bhagwat of the Open University. Special thanks to Kew's Gina Fullerlove and Mark Nesbitt, to Jim Endersby for commenting on the entire text and to Craig Brough and Kew's library and archives team for helping locate publications during the research process.

The publishing team at the Royal Botanic Gardens, Kew would like to thank all of the above and in addition Lynn Parker, Julia Buckley and other members of Kew's Library, Art and Archives team; Kew photographers Paul Little and Andrew McRobb; Jane Ellison, Katie Pollard, Adrian Washbourne and Jen Whyntie at the BBC; Georgina Laycock, Caroline Westmore, Juliet Brightmore, Sara Marafini and Amanda Jones at John Murray; Heather Angel,

ACKNOWLEDGEMENTS

Begoña Aguirre-Hudson, Christine Beard, Elaine Charwat, Tim Harris, Christopher Mills, Laura Martinez-suz, Lynn Modaberi, Vicky Murphy, Sarah Philips, Anna Quenby, Greg Redwood, Shirley Sherwood, Michiel van Slageren, Rhian Smith and Maria Vorontsova. Very special thanks go to the author team, Kathy Willis, Carolyn Fry, Norman Miller and Emma Townshend, for making this book project possible.

ILLUSTRATION CREDITS

All images are © Board of Trustees of the Royal Botanic Gardens, Kew unless otherwise stated below.

Colour plate sections: 1/4 above, © The Trustees of The Natural History Museum, London; 1/4 below, by permission of the Linnean Society of London; 2/1 below, Michael Graham-Stewart/Bridgeman Art Library; 2/7, *Angraecum sesquipedale* by Judi Stone; 3/1 above right and below, Colin Clubbe; 3/3 above, National Gallery London/Bridgeman Art Library; 3/3 below, Leslie Garland Picture Library/Alamy; 4/1 above and below, Henk Beentje; 4/3, John Dransfield; 4/8 above, Heather Angel/Natural Visions; 4/8 below, Laura Martinez-suz.

Every reasonable effort has been made to trace copyright holders, but if there are any errors or omissions, John Murray will be pleased to insert the appropriate acknowledgement in any subsequent printings or editions.

Icon illustrations: 1, Rudbeck woodcut of *Linnaea borealis*; 2, Wardian case, for growing ferns; 3, stamp marking William Hooker's herbarium sheets at Kew; 4, potato, from John Gerard's *Herbal or General Historie of Plantes*, 1633; 5, *Phormium tenax*, the New Zealand flax; 6, Annie Paxton standing on *Victoria amazonica* leaf; 7, rubber seedling (*Hevea brasiliensis*); 8, *Stanhopea* orchid in the wild, from James Bateman's *The Orchidaceae of Mexico and Guatemala*, 1837–43; 9, *Lantana camara*, invasive plant, native of South America; 10, Gregor Mendel; 11, microscope, engraved illustration, 1889; 12, adder's tongue fern (*Ophioglossum*), a record-breaking polyploid, having 96 sets of chromosomes; 13, European elm bark beetle (*Scolytus multistriatus*); 14, Bright wheat, from John Gerard's *Herbal or General Historie of Plantes*, 1633; 15, packets of quinine from India, each containing five grains of pure quinine, commonly sold at post offices; 16, illustration from Charles Darwin's *The Movements and Habits of Climbing Plants*, 1876; 17, *Nymphaea thermarum*, the Rwandan pigmy waterlily, by Lucy T. Smith; 18, acorns and oak leaves from John

Gerard's *Herbal or General Historie of Plantes*, 1633; 19, *Centaurea melitensis* seeds; 20, *Arabidopsis thaliana*; 21, tree of plant evolution; 22, palm from Roxburgh Collection, painted in Calcutta; 23, globe, engraved illustration, 1851; 24, detail from sacred Hindu grove near Chandod on the banks of the Narmada river, 1782; 25, engraving of bee pollinating flower.

FURTHER READING

Allan, Mea, *The Hookers of Kew, 1785–1911*, Michael Joseph, 1967

Banks, Joseph, *The Journal of Joseph Banks in the Endeavour, 1768–1771*, Genesis Publications, 1980

Banks, R.E.R., Elliott, B., Hawkes, J.G., King-Hele, D. and Lucas, G.L. (eds), *Sir Joseph Banks: A Global Perspective*, Royal Botanic Gardens, Kew, 1994

Bateman, James, *The Orchidaceae of Mexico & Guatemala*, Ridgway & Sons, 1837–43

Blunt, Wilfrid, *Linnaeus: The Compleat Naturalist*, Frances Lincoln, 2004

Brasier, Clive, 'New Horizons in Dutch Elm Disease Control', *Report on Forest Research*, HMSO, 1996

Chambers, Neil (ed.), *Scientific Correspondence of Sir Joseph Banks, 1765–1820*, Pickering and Chatto, 2007

Colquhoun, Kate, *'The Busiest Man in England': A Life of Joseph Paxton, Gardener, Architect and Victorian Visionary*, Fourth Estate, 2006

Craft, Paul, Riffle, Robert Lee and Zona, Scott, *The Encyclopedia of Cultivated Palms*, Timber Press, 2012

Darwin, Charles, *On the Origin of Species by Means of Natural Selection*, John Murray, 1859

Desmond, Ray, *Sir Joseph Dalton Hooker: Traveller and Plant Collector*, Antique Collectors' Club, 1999

—— , *The History of the Royal Botanic Gardens, Kew*, 2nd edn, Royal Botanic Gardens, Kew, 2007

Dransfield, John, Uhl, Natalie W., Asmussen, Conny B., Baker, William J., Harley, Madeline M. and Lewis, Carl E., *Genera Palmarum: The Evolution and Classification of Palms*, 2nd edn, Royal Botanic Gardens, Kew, 2008

Endersby, Jim, *A Guinea Pig's History of Biology: The Animals and Plants Who Taught Us the Facts of Life*, William Heinemann, 2007

—— , *Imperial Nature: Joseph Hooker and the Practices of Victorian Science*, Chicago, IL: University of Chicago Press, 2008

—— , *Orchid*, Reaktion Books (forthcoming)

Flanagan, Mark and Kirkham, Tony, *Wilson's China: A Century On*, Royal Botanic Gardens, Kew, 2009

Fry, Carolyn, *The World of Kew*, BBC Books, 2006

—— , *The Plant Hunters: The Adventures of the World's Greatest Botanical Explorers*, Andre Deutsch, 2009

——, Seddon, Sue and Vines, Gail, *The Last Great Plant Hunt: The Story of Kew's Millennium Seed Bank*, Royal Botanic Gardens, Kew, 2011

Greene, E.L., *Landmarks of Botanical History*, Redwood City, CA: Stanford University Press, 1983

Griggs, Patricia, *Joseph Hooker: Botanical Trailblazer*, Royal Botanic Gardens, Kew, 2011

Harberd, Nicholas, *Seed to Seed: The Secret Life of Plants*, Bloomsbury, 2006

Holway, Tatiana, *The Flower of Empire: An Amazonian Water Lily, the Quest to Make it Bloom, and the World it Created*, Oxford University Press, 2013

Honigsbaum, Mark, *The Fever Trail: The Hunt for the Cure for Malaria*, Macmillan, 2001

Hoyles, M., *The Story of Gardening*, Journeyman, 1991

Jarvis, Charlie, *Order Out of Chaos: Linnaean Plant Names and Their Types*, Linnean Society of London, 2007

Jeffreys, Diarmuid, *Aspirin: The Remarkable Story of a Wonder Drug*, Bloomsbury, 2004

Kingsbury, Noël, *Hybrid: The History and Science of Plant Breeding*, Chicago, IL: University of Chicago Press, 2009

Koerner, Lisbet, *Linnaeus: Nature and Nation*, Cambridge, MA: Harvard University Press, 1999

Lack, H. Walter and Baker, William J., *The World of Palms*, Berlin: Botanischer Garten und Botanisches Museum Berlin-Dahlem, 2011

Loadman, John, *Tears of the Tree: The Story of Rubber – A Modern Marvel*, Oxford University Press, 2005

Loskutov, Igor, G., *Vavilov and His Institute: A History of the World Collection of Plant Genetic Resources in Russia*, Rome: International Plant Genetic Resources Institute, 1999

Mawer, Simon, *Gregor Mendel: Planting the Seeds of Genetics*, New York: Abrams, 2006

Money, Nicholas P., *The Triumph of the Fungi: A Rotten History*, Oxford University Press, 2007

Morgan, J. and Richards, A., *A Paradise Out of a Common Field: The Pleasures and Plenty of the Victorian Garden*, Century, 1990

Morton, Alan G., *History of Botanical Science: An Account of the Development of Botany from Ancient Times to the Present Day*, Academic Press, 1981

Nabhan, Gary Paul, *Where Our Food Comes From: Retracing Nikolay Vavilov's Quest to End Famine*, Island Press, 2009

Pringle, Peter, *The Murder of Nikolai Vavilov: The Story of Stalin's*

Persecution of One of the Great Scientists of the Twentieth Century, Simon and Schuster, 2008

Saunders, G., *Picturing Plants: An Analytical History of Botanical Illustration*, 2nd edn, Chicago, IL: University of Chicago Press, 2009

Schiebinger, L., *Plants and Empire: Colonial Bioprospecting in the Atlantic World*, Cambridge, MA: Harvard University Press, 2004

Schumann, Gail Lynn, *Hungry Planet: Stories of Plant Diseases*, St Paul, MN: APS Press, 2012

Suttor, George, *Memoirs Historical and Scientific of the Right Honourable Joseph Banks, BART*, Parramatta, NSW: E. Mason, 1855

Turrill, W.B., *Pioneer Plant Geography: The Phytogeographical Researches of Sir Joseph Dalton Hooker*, The Hague: Martinus Nijhoff, 1953

Weber, Ewald, *Invasive Plant Species of the World: A Reference Guide to Environmental Weeds*, CABI Publishing, 2003

Willis, Kathy and McElwain, Jennifer, *The Evolution of Plants*, Oxford University Press, 2013

Online Resources

Darwin Correspondence Project: http://www.darwinproject.ac.uk/

Darwin Online: http://darwin-online.org.uk

Joseph Hooker Correspondence: http://www.kew.org/science-conservation/collections/joseph-hooker

Royal Botanic Gardens, Kew: http://www.kew.org

INDEX

Numerals in italic denote illustrations